Life Elements

Transform Your Life With Earth, Air, Fire, and Water

Izolda Trakhtenberg

Healer's Arts Publishing
Greenbelt, Maryland

Life Elements: Transform Your Life With Earth, Air, Fire, and Water © 2008, Izolda Trakhtenberg

Cover design: Alexander Bradley, Cover photography by FreeStockPhotos.com and www.bigfotos.com.

Published by Healer's Arts Publishing, PO Box 1133, Greenbelt, MD 20768 http://www.healersarts.com. Printed in the U.S.A.

Trakhtenberg, Izolda d.1966-

Life Elements: Transform your life with earth, air, fire, and water/ Izolda Trakhtenberg; 1st. ed.

Summary: The "Life Elements" system helps you reach within yourself, to figure out and direct your own progression toward integration, wholeness, and joy through cultivating the four elements, Earth, Air, Fire, and Water.

256p. cm.
ISBN: 978-0-9802298-0-6

1. Self- improvement. 2. New Age Movement 3. Self-perception. 4. Meditation-Internet resources 5. Philosophy-Mind and body.

I. Trakhtenberg, Izolda. II. Title.

Dewey class: 158.12

10 9 8 7 6 5 4 3 2 1

Contents

Illustrations

Acknowledgments

Many people took an active role in the creation of this book. First, I wish to thank all those wonderful people who helped test the assessment tools and for being sounding boards for my ideas and the first explorers of some of the Missions and Meditations: Elissa, Gina, Betsy, Joe, Dave, Diane, Alec, Terry, Melissa, Petra, Janet, Jessica, Renée, Alex, Sean, Lee, Cora, Dan, Kristin, William, Tucker, Koralleen, Leana, Rraine, Lee, Kathy, Winston, Nell, Emily, Emily F., Sara, Sondra, Kristen, and Rich.

To the authors Deepak Chopra, Shakti Gawain, Dan Milman, Rodney Yee, Starhawk, Madeline Bruser, Joan Bunning, and Julia Cameron who have guided me on my path.

I owe a great big thank-you to Kristin Matherly for her wonderful work on developing and programming the website for the online version of the assessment tools. She was invaluable in creating a wonderful and user-friendly site.

I also want to thank Alexander Bradley, whose beautiful design graces the cover, Arlene Robinson for stellar editing, and Jeanne Robin for creating the cataloguing information.

To Sondra, Lara, Kristen, Terry, and Paula for their friendship, their boundless enthusiasm and their love.

I am grateful to my sister Emily Altman, M.D., without whose support and ideas this book would never have been published.

To the amazing Tempest, Pyro, and Kimba for their loyalty and patience as I completed this manuscript.

My wonderful husband Rich Potter, for his unfailing support and love and the magic of our life together.

My clients and students. It is through my work with them that these theories and practices have developed. The tried-and-true Missions and Meditations in this book were created and developed to help people find and walk their paths.

Last, I thank you who have embarked on this process. Look inside yourself. Find your highest truth, and then follow your own lead. You will make yourself proud.

Chapter 1
Where Are We Now and How Did We Get Here?

"Why didn't I stand up for myself?" Janet asks as she leaves her boss's office. "I knew Sharon was somehow going to take credit for my presentation, but I just couldn't say anything!"

Why can't I make a decision between these two phones? Ben thinks while he stands in the store. *It always takes me forever to make up my mind. I can't even decide on the best way to decide!*

"Why do I keep doing these one-night stands?" Cheryl asks herself. "How do I always seem to find myself in these situations?"

Janet, Ben and Cheryl all have something in common. They feel there is something missing from their lives, but they are not sure what that "something" might be. Also, they all want a better grasp on how they can be their best: how they can move in the world with certainty, peace, and happiness. But, they feel as though at least some parts of their lives are a mystery. Oh, they might achieve success in some aspects, but achievement in others remains elusive.

Perhaps similar thoughts drew you to pick up this book. Like Janet, have you been having feelings of sadness or dissatisfaction?

Or, have you been feeling the same kind of emptiness or lethargy Ben is feeling, making it difficult for him to make a simple decision?

Like Cheryl, do you find yourself jumping into relationship after relationship without stopping to decide about what you *really* want in a partner? Or perhaps you drift from one relationship to the next, yet never truly feel settled in any of them?

It is true that, sometimes, we all simply feel adrift. We focus too much on how others see or treat us, and can be easily hurt as a result. Or, we might find it incredibly difficult to accept decisions we know would be good and healthy for us. Other times, we find it hard to act on healthy decisions we have already made. Ironically, we might not find it difficult at all to act on decisions that work against our best interests, especially when those decisions continue already established patterns of behavior. Still other times we feel unstable, unable to reach a sense of peace and equilibrium.

The scenarios mentioned above occur often and to many people. The questions above are asked by many who seek answers about how to live better lives. So many of us walk in this world without being fully present in our lives. We go to jobs that might or might not satisfy us. We endure relationships that feel hollow and unfulfilling, all the while rationalizing why we persist in staying. We allow our very passionate and creative natures to wither away as we strive to create a day-to-day idealized world that is actually rather impossible to achieve.

I believe that we tend to buy into the media culture. We spend so much of our time being pummeled with marketing ideas that we are not enough and that we do not have enough. Further, we receive the message that unless we do what the commercial says, we will never reach these goals that are quite likely unreachable in the first place.

These ideas are presented to us in every magazine and every television show and commercial. Interestingly, they are presented as if the world they describe is the real world. The beautiful woman on the television show, who somehow juggles her corporate law profession, two children, a husband, and all of her friends' problems, still somehow manages to cook, clean, work out, have a terrific figure and show up for her daughter's fourth-grade play. She also manages to win the case, do volunteer work and perhaps even take care of her ailing mother.

Is this a realistic scenario? Can this superwoman really exist in our world? Or, is it perhaps too much to expect of anyone? I believe that since we see it occur as something commonplace on so many television shows and movies, we have come to expect these accomplishments of ourselves. The insidious thing is, not only do we expect to accomplish all of these tasks, we expect to complete them brilliantly. Then, when we do not complete everything we expect of ourselves, many of us begin to believe that we are the ones at fault. We blame ourselves for our inability to do all that others seem to accomplish, and this internalization of feelings of inadequacy can lead to depression, or worse.

It is no wonder that so many of us live feeling unhappy and dissatisfied. As long as we are bombarded with these impossible images, and as long as we believe they are possible and that we are somehow deficient if we do not achieve them, we contribute to and support a system that, in some ways, is designed to make our lives more challenging than they were ever destined to be.

I believe there is a new and different way to approach our lives. In hunting for the perfect partner, the perfect car, house or job, we lose sight of so much that might already be good and bountiful in our lives. We lose sight of the simplest of nature's gifts that can teach us so very much. We spend such large amounts of time striving for benchmarks of success; we might not realize or credit ourselves with the many successes we have already achieved. When we analyze our achievements and compare them to those of others, we feel we fall short. This happens in part because we follow guidelines set forth from people and institutions outside ourselves.

Basically, it is like this: We have all these outside sources that tell us what we need to do and be to be happy. The problem is that, for so many of us, we strive and we achieve the things we were told we must achieve, and then when we look around, we find we still are not settled or happy in our lives. To me, it makes perfect sense that so many climb the mountain, only to find they remain unhappy when they look around once they get there. This happens because these people have been looking to someone else to tell them what will be right for them. If this message has been coming from external sources, then when we make changes, they are to satisfy an external requirement. They do not come from within. We wait for someone else to approve of what we have achieved, and for the most part, we do not stop to think about what *we* want and what *we* might do for ourselves that would help us move toward happiness, peace, and joy in our lives.

I wrote this book to offer a new and different approach to finding some of that peace and joy. The "Life Elements" system helps you reach within yourself, to figure out and direct your own progression toward integration, wholeness, and joy. The Elements Earth, Air, Fire, and Water, and their cultivation, are the means by which you will accomplish this Integration Process. To quote the amazing Helen Keller, "Life is either a daring adventure or nothing." The Elements Earth, Air, Fire, and Water will be there to help you on this grand adventure where the destination is your peace, joy, and transformation.

I wish you joy and success in this wonderful process of discovery. Through the Life Elements System, you will assess where you are now, and then you will create the road map to your own mountaintop. Through your own direction and the enclosed Missions and Meditations, you will choose how you will transform your life.

Note: Where appropriate, the introductions to some of the Missions provide a list of all of the items you will need to complete them. However, one of the most important things you will need to complete the Integration Process is some sort of notebook or three-ring binder, in which you can write your thoughts, feelings, and ideas about this especially personal and intimate journey. This will be your Life Elements Journal.

Chapter 2
Now Is The Time

Recently, people have been looking for new ways of living. Websites such as the Simple Living Network (http://www. simpleliving.net/main/), and techniques such as Reiki and other energy healing methods have proliferated on the Internet, in daily life, and in our consciousness. Some of these methods have become popular across the gamut of our culture and society. Many of us want to take control of our lives and destinies and move in the world in our own way and on our own terms. We seek answers in innovative and unusual arenas because the standard answers no longer resonate with many of us; they no longer feel relevant. Many have tried to follow the prescribed guidelines of the media culture, yet many have begun to believe there must be another way—a way that allows for joy and fulfillment without the constant pressure brought on by outside expectations.

Now, today, it is time to forge our own paths to a fulfilling, bountiful existence. In addition to the relatively new Internet culture that gives access to so much information, including websites like the Simple Living Network mentioned above, many are turning to older ways, and are incorporating relevant aspects of those ways into their lives. Many are, in fact, combining facets of a number of different methods to forge their own paths. The combination of many factors allows greater access to sources for a peaceful and joyful existence.

One of our gifts as a species is that we are free to choose what works for us. So often, we hear about people who use the Internet and other cutting-edge technologies, and who are also practitioners of the ancient practices of yoga or Tai Chi. These ancient health and wellness systems are being reinvigorated and reinterpreted for our modern age. Witness the popularity of both yoga and Tai Chi. To be a bit flippant, you can't swing a yoga mat without bumping into a yoga studio. Gyms and health clubs all over the world have embraced these ancient teachings and brought them out of the *ashrams* (yogic temples) and *dojos* (martial art studios) and into the mainstream. Yoga classes teach the strength, flexibility and focus necessary for fitness as well as the more spiritual aspects of yoga's teachings. The same can be said for Tai Chi. Tai Chi teaches balance, fitness, and peace. Many parks host contemporary Tai Chi practitioners daily.

These arts have also incorporated key teachings where the natural world plays a vital role. In fact, it can be said that each relies on nature for its inspiration. In Tai Chi, everything is cyclical. A Tai Chi form flows along a prescribed set of motions and postures, and it ends exactly where it began. The postures flow and repeat in a manner not unlike the changing of the seasons, yet the wheel of the form and the wheel of the year change and progress. In Tai Chi, "There is no up without a down. There is no left without a right." These sentences both relate quite strongly to Newton's Laws of Motion, and natural law itself. In Tai Chi, one ends at the beginning, and natural forces that flow in a form create a symbiotic relationship to the practitioner who does not fight nature, but rather allows him or herself to be carried along like a leaf on a stream.

Yoga, too, embraces nature in many ways. From the imitation of animal forms in yoga *asanas*, or postures (and the spirit of the animal energetically) to the spiritual bond that is formed with nature through a yoga practice, the natural world plays a large role in this ancient system. In addition, yoga celebrates the universal connection of the *prana,* or life force of the individual, to the life force of the universe.

Both yoga and Tai Chi are ancient arts. Their resurgence has in part reawakened a thirst for the wisdom of early teachings. These practices are as vital today as they were in ancient times, and there is another system of study that is remarkably relevant to our world. I am speaking of something that is both ancient, and that has had a resurgence of renewed interest over the last thirty or so years.

Nature obviously comes in many forms, but to the ancients,

our ancestors, nature came in only four basic forms, and everything on our planet could be divided into these four Elemental forms, or Elements. These Elements were Earth, Air, Fire, and Water, and they played a vital role in both our development as peoples and our development as individuals.

Since everything the ancients saw and knew was relatively easily categorized into one of these four Elements, the Elements became powerful symbols. If everything could be said to be part of one or more of the Elements, then the Elements must be responsible for a great deal of what went on in history. In fact, we even have expressions that say that we are "at the mercy of the elements" (being caught in a storm, for example). In addition to being the building blocks of everything, over time, the Elements became synonymous with and symbolic for categories of existence as well. Certain personality traits, for example, became relegated to different Elements. So, someone who had a volatile personality was said to have a "fiery" or Fire personality. With the development of astrology, the Elements became more formally distributed among the zodiac signs, and personality traits were established and studied according to those signs.

Despite the fact that many have believed in and followed the teachings of astrology, this book does not intend to detail astrology. My intent here is to acknowledge that astrology has used the Elements extensively to categorize personality traits and characteristics. Other systems of wellness have also used the Elements, and these include the Chinese art of acupuncture, and Ayurveda from India. All these systems attempt to identify issues of wellness and address them while making use of Elemental energies in one form or another. These Elemental energies have been used to illuminate and aid both physical and psychological health. They have also helped answer questions of identity and personality. In other words, they give us glimpses into who we are and perhaps why we are here.

"Who am I? Why am I here? What is my role in the world?" These questions are enduring; at one point or another, almost everyone on their life's journey seeks the answers. Many books have been written on this subject, and the self-help aisle of many bookstores overflows with possible paths. Churches, synagogues, and other spiritual organizations also attempt to give answers to these questions. Other avenues to pursue in addition to the above are the teachings of Native American spirituality, psychology in the form of personality theory, and astrology. Of these schools of thought, a number look to the ancient Elements of Earth, Air, Fire, and Water for answers. As I stated above, ancient peoples believed that everything was created out of these four Elements. A number of historical records indicate that some alchemists who lived in the Middle Ages believed these four Elements comprised everything on the Earth and were necessary for survival.

To simplify physical science a great deal, it could be said that everything comes symbolically from either one or a combination of Elements. All mineral-based elements can be traced back to the earth. The air we breathe needs little explanation: without it, one can only survive a scarce few minutes. Water, which gives life and from which life comes, is vital to everyone's survival. Fire, whether it is the flame in the hearth, the destructive but sometimes necessary burn of a wildfire, or the heat of the noonday sun, gives life-sustaining energy and heat. We can symbolically attribute almost anything in our world to one or more of these four Elements. In turn, the Elements govern that which they represent. For more on these topics, please see the individual chapters on each Element.

We are not discussing inorganic and organic chemistry when I say that all of the Periodic Elements come from the earth. What I am saying is that the Earth Element symbolizes these elements: minerals, soil, trees, mountains, stones, and crystals. In other words, the Earth Element represents the physical world of the earth. In addition, the Water Element represents the physical world of oceans, streams, brooks, seas, lakes, rain, and the water we drink. The Fire Element represents the flame in the hearth, the fireplace, the bonfire, the wildfire, the candle flame, and the sun. The Air Element represents the atmosphere, the air we breathe, and that which resides above us. So, when I write of the Elements, these are the Elements about which I speak. The Elements are symbols for the myriad aspects of life on our planet. They have been described, analyzed, and incorporated into myth and legend for millennia. And they are still full of mystery and knowledge for us to seek out and learn from today.

In addition to stating that everything on the planet can be attributed symbolically to one or more of the four Elements, I will go so far as to say that all living beings are also made up of these Elements. Every part of each person can be categorized as being part of one or more of the Elements. Our breath is Air, of course. Our blood and other fluids are Water. Our skeleton, muscles, cartilage, and other physical substance can symbolize Earth. Last, Fire symbolizes the electrical impulses that move along our nervous system, fire neurons in the brain, and actually propel us forward.

We, too, are made up of the Elements. Thus, since we can establish our own bodies being delineated Elementally, it is not a stretch to assert that the Elements can also govern our nonphysical selves. Astrology has already made the assertions about personality characteristics and their relationships to the Elements, so I will not detail this here. Simply, if the Elements govern certain broad spectra of personality types, then we can systematically identify and assess those traits, and then work with them to create a healthier and richer way of living.

Like ancient cultures that followed the cycles and seasons of the year, many today follow the principles indicated by yoga, Tai Chi, Ayurveda, astrology, and feng shui. We draw inspiration from these ancient principles, and from the cultural mores that were passed from generation to generation. Some of these mores have survived as superstitions, some have remained as cultural norms, but a large number are treated as simply the manner in which we do things.

While many cultures have influenced our development to our present state, a few had more impact than others did. The lives of these ancient peoples served as lessons to their modern-day counterparts. Each of the following cultures honored the Elements in various ways. Each culture attributed characteristics to the four Elements. The Babylonians, Greeks and Romans developed what is now modern astrology. In India, the Hindus developed Ayurveda, which also depicts Elemental energies with respect to Earth, Air, Fire, and Water. In China, the healing practices of acupuncture and acupressure, also over 5,000 years old, honored and worked with the elements of earth, fire, water, metal, and wood.

In an effort to make sense of their lives and their world, ancient peoples developed myths to explain much of what they needed to identify and name. Like all cultures, and people in general, the people of ancient Greece and Rome wanted to categorize the world around them. They needed to explain things like the seasons, birth, death, survival, and the very reasons for their existence. They also developed methods of describing and categorizing relevant information. Once they developed these explanations, I believe they then began to see the need to explain people and their behaviors. They did so with myths and legends and the constellations. Edith Hamilton's *Mythology* is an excellent resource for both Greek and Roman myths and legends.

For millennia, people have looked up to the sky for answers. The heavens are said to be above us. The sky holds endless mystery. The stars hold secrets for us to seek and find. The ancients saw the stars and they created the constellations as guideposts on the way to finding answers. The constellations were given the names of Greek and Roman gods and mythological characters. These characters told the tales and history of the people.

Other constellations were given governance over the characteristics of those people born when those constellations sailed across the night sky. The twelve constellations that make up the zodiac, for example, all played a part in the development and characterization of people. For thousands of years, astrologers have looked at the signs of the zodiac and have created charts based on the twelve signs and their ruling planets. Each sign of the zodiac has certain distinct personality traits. Each sign also has an Element associated with it. These Elements are also named Earth, Air, Fire, and Water. In broad terms, each Element is connected to three zodiac signs. For example, Aquarius, Libra, and Gemini are Air signs. Cancer, Scorpio, Pisces are Water signs. Aries, Leo, and Sagittarius are Fire signs. Taurus, Virgo, and Capricorn are Earth signs. Since the signs are governed by specific Elements, people born under those signs exhibit the traits associated with those Elements.

Many people today look to astrology, Ayurveda, or Chinese astrology for guidance and answers about their lives, traits, and tendencies. However, I recognize that we are all individuals, and are products of our past and life experiences. Our experiences have shaped us, and to a great extent, inform who we are today. In fact, some people might say that because of their histories and the baggage they carry from those histories, it is extremely challenging for them to get to a better place. These people might believe that the patterns that have been established are permanent, and might be impossible to dislodge or modify. Other people might be in a great deal of pain, and therefore feel powerless to effect change in their lives in a permanent and beneficial manner. In other words, the well of their experience and pain feels bottomless. Thus, when they attempt even to see the pain, they find themselves drowning in it, and therefore the grief itself feels insurmountable.

I disagree that it is impossible to deal with and handle pain in its historical perspective. Certainly, we all have traumas, both historic and immediate, that affect our lives. Once again, I do agree with those who say that our experiences shape us and that it might be difficult to make significant change. Many different types of traumas might have affected our lives. While I am not going to list them here, please know that I do recognize that these traumas can be debilitating and devastating. And yet, I maintain that despite whatever traumas we have had in our lives, we are indeed still here. For whatever reason, we did not give up or give in. *We fought, we persevered, and we survived.*

Right now, please take a moment to acknowledge your survival and credit yourself with coming this far. Somehow, by hook or by crook as they say, you managed to get to this point. To honor this accomplishment, I will ask you to complete the following meditation. Please put the book down and sit comfortably (To access the audio version of this Meditation online, please click "Credit Yourself With How Far You've Come" in the Meditations section on the Life Elements website: http://www.LifeElements.info. The password is "peace" without the quotes.)

Once you are comfortable, take three deep, cleansing breaths. As you inhale, feel your entire body expanding up and out, and as you exhale, feel your body gently float back into itself. Allow your mind to quiet as you do this. Let your thoughts float gently through you as you breathe.

If you find yourself starting to think of something in particular, I encourage you to tell yourself that you will come back to that thought later, but that this time, this moment is just for you. You are the sum of all you have survived. Your past has formed you, and you are here right now. When you feel ready, say the words, "I survived. I am still here."

You might wish to repeat the words a few more times. As you do so, keep breathing deeply. Sit for a moment and contemplate all you have done to get here, today. And in fact, not only did you survive, but you also managed to get to a place where you are ready for the next step. Instead of simple and vital survival, you are now ready to learn how to thrive.

You might find old thoughts coming up, and the strength of your reaction to this Meditation might surprise you. Please try to stay in your deep breathing, and simultaneously see if you can mentally step back and peacefully acknowledge and assess those thoughts. See if you can identify exactly what you feel as you sit here, now. More importantly, try to look for a sense of peace about your current state. Remember, you have arrived here, at this point in time and space, so you can create the life you choose.

Maintain your deep breathing while you slowly allow yourself once again to become aware of the space around you. Become aware of the outside world as you bring yourself back to the here and now. When you are ready, open your eyes. (Please note that you might have some reactions to this Meditation. If so, I encourage you to write them down in your Life Elements Journal.)

I submit to you that the very strengths that helped you to get to this point will also stand you in good stead as you undertake this new journey. Regardless of where you have been, you are here now, and I believe that you are ready to make changes in your life. You can change what everyone expects, including what you yourself expect, by deciding that you will do so. That moment of decision becomes critical to this process. That one moment of decision gives us a new lease, because once it has been made, the decision allows us to modify how we act and react, so that we are now living on our own terms. While we might never fully remove our historically ingrained instinctive responses, we can certainly add new and different ways to think, be, do and feel, so they become almost second nature. Once those new ways of being become more accessible, we will then be able to usher in a new way of living, because we will have so many more options.

One of the things I wish to accomplish with this book is to help you take control of your life so that you live both with purpose, and on purpose. I honor you for getting here.

Chapter 3
What Is The Life Elements System?

Now that we have talked a bit about the cultural and historic perspective of the Elements and honored our own perspective and current status, let us look more closely at the Elements themselves.

As you have learned, some ancient cultures used the Elements to explain, describe, and even predict patterns of behavior. In astrology, the Elements have been given governance of various specific categories of personality traits. For example, each of the Air signs has traits in common. Common wisdom in astrology says that Air signs tend to be the thought-oriented people. They value sound judgment, intelligence, thought, reasoning, and logic. They do not tend to be ruled by their emotions, but instead allow their intellect to guide them through life. Fire people tend to be passionate, quick to act or react, active people who are always in motion. Earth Element-ruled people tend to be more practical and centered than their counterparts. Water people tend to be ruled by their emotions and intuition. Broadly, the Elements that govern their birth signs determine their basic personality types.

In astrology, as in Ayurveda, once you have these signs/planets ruling your personality, you are generally seen in this light for the rest of your life. Ayurveda is more proactive, in that people cultivate *ayurvedic* strengths by attempting to balance the Vata, Pitta and Kapha bodily humours (also known as *doshas*). However, for the most part, a person's personality and body type are set, and will not change fundamentally. Yet, life is a dynamic and ever-changing process, and as it changes, so can we change. Sometimes these transformations are brought upon us, and sometimes we make changes in our own lives. The Life Elements System takes your current status, your personality type and strengths, and builds upon them. With Life Elements, you will be able to expand your self-knowledge and actions in a way that allows you to live wholly.

Regardless of the circumstances, I believe that we can make great and broad changes in the ways we instinctively approach new challenges. For example, if we are thought-oriented Air personalities, we might instinctively approach a dilemma with our thinking caps on. We might not immediately gravitate toward an emotional/intuitive solution, because it is not our immediate reaction. Although an intuitive reaction might not be our immediate response, we can teach ourselves to give one when it is appropriate. If, as stated above, we accept that we are symbolically created of all of the Elements, and if we accept that these four Elements correspond to various personality characteristics, then we can accept the possibility that the various characteristics governed by those four Elements can be available to us, because they already exist inside us. The basic idea is this: *If we are made up of all the Elements, then why can't we have access to all of them?*

I believe the strengths of all four Elements reside in us, even if they are not outwardly present. If we are indeed symbolically made of Earth, Air, Fire, and Water, then ultimately, every characteristic of these Elements can be ours to employ at appropriate moments in our lives. This is similar to the idea that since we are of both man and woman born, we have both masculine and feminine aspects. A common example is when a man might get in touch with his feminine side, or when a woman who wants to achieve in sports is considered a tomboy. Other examples are when a woman breaks through the glass ceiling to take on a more stereotypically male career, or when a woman works to be more assertive in a manner that has traditionally been part of male personality traits.

Put another way, if we all have both a feminine and a masculine aspect to our personalities, then we can access, use, and make peace with each of those parts of ourselves. The same can be said for the Elements. Thus, even if we are thought-oriented Air personalities, we can still access our innate intuition (a Water quality) regardless of whether we exhibit intuitive Water abilities in our everyday lives.

We can still truly feel our emotions, even if our first instinct is to think things through rather than to feel them. So, even if someone is primarily an Air personality, she or he can still cultivate aspects of the other Elements to form a well-rounded way of living.

This is the key of the Life Elements System. We have more freedom to move in the world than we might believe we possess. We are not bound by where we currently stand. Some paradigms would have us believe that our current status is static: that we cannot fundamentally change our instinctive responses. However, I believe this structure is too limiting. I believe it is not necessary for us to content ourselves with our present status. We can change it. We do not have to live with the reasoning of Air or the impetuousness of Fire as if they are the only game in town, as it were. Even if these responses come immediately and instinctively because those Elements most closely govern us, we can still change how we react if we take steps to modify how we approach new situations.

For example, even if we are Air or Fire personalities, we will find ourselves in situations when the more centered approach of Earth or the intuition of Water will be a more beneficial response. We might perhaps find ourselves needing to sit and be at peace with a situation instead of jumping up and reacting immediately. Or, we might need to find our innate compassion to resolve an issue that previously might have elicited a thought-out response that lacked empathy or even sympathy.

To respond in a manner that is for the highest good of all, we might need to change old behaviors that have previously proved unsatisfactory. The basic premise is this: Instead of continuing on a path of repeating patterns that feel unfulfilling or limiting, we can take control of our internal processes and cultivate new responses, new ideas, and ultimately, new ways of living.

Several methods of personality assessment, and even ones that rely on Elemental energies for explanations, would have us believe we are the most developed we will be, and nothing can be done to change us fundamentally. However, the Life Elements System proposes that indeed, we can make those primary changes in ourselves. When we are faced with a situation where the fluidity, flexibility, and emotional awareness of Water are necessary, we can gain access to the strengths of Water. We can then use those attributes for the greater good, both for ourselves and for the world around us, even if those parts of ourselves seem hidden or untapped. Or, if the center and stability of the Earth Element will be the best influence in a situation, we can learn how to access those attributes when the need for them arises.

The method for doing this is the heart of the Life Elements System; we can grow in our strengths in the Elements, and thereby become fully well-rounded individuals who can take control of our lives and guide ourselves on our own paths. So, in an instance where Water characteristics are beneficial in resolving a situation, we can do so if we have cultivated Water Element qualities. Then, we can increasingly rely on those qualities to the point where they will become second nature. We can do the same for all of the Elements, and that is what makes the Life Elements System different from any other system. With Life Elements, we take control of our lives and direct how we will progress on the Life Elements Integration Process. We complete the Missions and Meditations to actualize ourselves, and thereby build strength, certainty, and peace. We will find and walk our authentic path. The guides are the Missions and Meditations in the Life Elements System, and the destinations are our internal strengths.

Once we know where we wish to go, the Missions will help us start moving toward our goals. First, we must determine where we now stand. This means we have to ask and answer some internal questions about who we are right now and how we respond to the situations life brings us. Just as with astrology (learning about your sign and other aspects) and Ayurveda (the Vata-Pitta-Kapha body type assessment), we must assess our status. Then, we can make changes by cultivating the Elements we need.

If we begin to ask and answer questions about our own identity, we begin to increase our awareness of our motivations, responses, and behaviors. We also increase our awareness of our life path. With that new consciousness, we will begin to notice patterns. Some believe that once these patterns are ingrained, they are impossible to modify—that they are set in stone, as it were. However, this does not appear to be the case. Certainly, cognitive-behavioral therapists will agree that a pattern can be changed when the person with the pattern wants to change it. The person works on changing the pattern by modifying the behavior that maintains it until the pattern is altered. This is sometimes known as the "fake it 'til you make it" method.

It will take some work and a great deal of awareness on the part of the person wishing to make modifications, yet it is certainly possible for this to be accomplished. So, when we wish to make a change, we repattern our usual responses to situations. Once we begin the repatterning process, we can then modify not only how we react to new stimuli, but also how we behave and how we approach and think through new ideas and new challenges. This repatterning process can take many forms, and often, people spend many years in counseling learning to modify their own behavior in a healthy and directed manner.

Although many rely on counseling to help them notice and modify their patterns, I believe it is possible for us to initiate these changes ourselves. If we increase our own awareness of our patterns, we can then begin to recognize behavior we might wish to change. Once that recognition occurs, we can then initiate small changes in our patterns while still keeping an eye on and evaluating the patterns as they occur. That is one of the reasons a Life Elements Journal will be crucial for you on this journey. Those changes will create a new pattern because of the ripple effect that occurs with the initial change. Like a pebble that is dropped in a still pond, all the water in the pond will eventually feel the impact. That one pebble, that one, minute change, will create waves that eventually affect all the water in the pond in some manner. It might not be visible immediately, but this change will come.

The water in the pond, being fluid, will stabilize to appear almost exactly the same, and we, in initiating change, might appear to stay exactly the same. However, on the microscopic scale, everything in the water is now different. The individual water molecules, the microorganisms, and the minerals in the water have all been displaced in one way or another by the ripple effect caused by the wave. When we make a change in our lives, even if it is a small change, we still modify the landscape of our lives. Similarly, our new awareness will likely have long-term repercussions in many aspects of our lives, even if the result is not immediately apparent. So, like the water in the pond, we are also different, because that one small change has made us so. The pattern of our lives will reorganize itself around this new paradigm, no matter its size. Then, as we become accustomed to this new way of being, we will likely find that larger changes will either become manifest, or can then be implemented in a healthy and fulfilling manner. By taking control of the changes in our lives, we allow for new energy to manifest in our lives. This new energy will bring us new experiences and new ways of seeing and being. This is an important distinction of the Life Elements System. Instead of *waiting* for change to come, we grab the proverbial bull by the horns and *initiate* change. This benefits us by making our lives the way we want them to be. More importantly, we take both the control and the responsibility for our lives into our own hands. The benefits of this to our self-esteem are great and myriad.

This entire process stems from the initial awareness of ourselves and our current state. Awareness is the greatest gift we can give to ourselves. With it comes self-assessment and eventual self-knowledge. Once we begin the self-assessment process, we become more self-aware, and then we can make changes as we find them necessary.

What follows is a brand-new system of actively assessing where you presently stand with respect to the Elemental characteristics and the roles they play in your life. Using the Element Designation Assessment Tool (EDAT) and the Element Imbalance Assessment Tool (EIAT), you assess where you stand now. Once you know that, through the use of Missions and Meditations, you can follow the appropriate steps to make permanent, positive changes. The Missions and Meditations will help you integrate the Elements, find your true path, and live your life fully. This is the Life Elements Integration Process.

Since you will complete these Missions at your own pace, you will find that your self-confidence increases with every one you finish. You will naturally gain something from each of these Missions, and they will change you elementally and fundamentally. As you symbolically strengthen your accessibility to the Elements, you will tangibly strengthen your ability to incorporate their characteristics into your life. This incorporation will change your worldview, and your perspective of your place in that worldview. The very fact that you have picked up this book indicates you are interested in finding something more—something authentic, and something that can help you change your life in a healthy, positive way. In addition, you will find that the changes you make are on your own terms. This is crucial, because changes initiated by the person, because of an understanding of where those changes are needed, make for a more long-lasting transformation.

Reading this book and completing the following Missions will change things for you. You will choose. You will become more aware. You will grow. And in these pages, you will meet and learn about your true self. These Missions and Meditations will enable you to trust yourself, to find a sense of peace, passion, and promise. Sometimes slowly, sometimes incredibly quickly, you will find yourself making changes in the way you respond to situations and in the way you live. You will no longer accept enduring pain or despair, because there will no longer be room for it in your new and more centered state. You will then live your "daring adventure."

Chapter 4
How Do We Make Changes?

How might we make changes in our lives? Certainly, we can go to therapy or counseling. It is one of the best methods of finding and keeping to a long-term path. We can also find psychics, astrologers, tarot readers, and many other people who will attempt to help us find our life paths. We might speak with friends, ministers, doctors, bosses, parents and other family members. These are all absolutely valid methods for determining the directions we wish our lives to go. However, of concern is that few, if any, of these methods allow for change to be driven by the person who seeks to make the change. All of these changes, in fact, seem to be sought by the seeker, but not necessarily made by that same seeker. Sure, there is much advice to be given, and certainly there is much to take in, but I believe that our individual organisms have a deep knowledge of what is right for us. We know inherently our correct course of action, and when we do not follow that course of action, we feel it deeply even if we do not acknowledge it overtly. We might not hear or listen to that internal voice that cautions us for or against a certain action, but often, if we slow down to listen, it is present. It is this internal voice we will attempt to engage through the Integration Process.

In the Life Elements System, the seeker chooses the correct path to integration. This might seem frightening, yet it is up to us to trust our internal voice here. We, each of us, have the strength to create fulfilling, contented lives, and we all know that few things in life are as satisfying as the completion of a project we began ourselves. Even if we are afraid to begin, once we do, we often find that things flow more smoothly than we expected. And, we reap the benefits of having initiated and completed a project in ways that are more than simply tangible. I cannot stress enough how much of an increase in self-esteem and self-confidence is derived from these kinds of actions. Here, you do it for yourself at your own prompting and impetus. You act because you motivate yourself, not at the insistence or cajoling of anyone else. The changes you make will end up more solid, because you have figured out the reasons why and satisfied your own need to know and grow.

In addition, the changes you make will be more genuine and more permanent. We are all individuals, and no one else ever truly sees our lives except us. No one can ever know our true thoughts and feelings, even though we might share them freely with others. I believe that we are such unique creatures, it is impossible for anyone to truly see what someone else is going through. Thus, when we make changes because we have decided to make them, they are more vital, more powerful, and more permanent.

There are so many sources telling us exactly how we should live our lives (exactly what we should be doing to get help), and yet unless the method "clicks" or feels right to us, it is only a temporary fix. Then, the danger exists that we will repeat patterns ingrained a long time ago and revert to old modes of behavior. With Life Elements, we ourselves evaluate where we are, and then develop our plan of action. This book provides you with options. You will evaluate your present status with the EDAT and the EIAT, and then complete the appropriate Missions and Meditations. You will develop your own process of completing the Missions. You will establish the timetable. You will take control. Then when you enact changes or embark on a particular path, these changes are more likely to stick.

Because we ourselves are the driving force behind the changes and because they make sense to us, patterns are more easily modified. No one will tell you exactly how to proceed. Your internal strength will enable you to make this decision and begin to act in the manner that best benefits your own growth and healing. I believe that once we breathe deeply and then take the reins of our lives in our hands and away from external sources, we can carve a new pattern for ourselves. We make a decision to enact a change, and therefore whenever we behave according to that planned change, we reinforce a way of being that makes sense to us. Thus, we can make it a new part of our lives that will remain established and integrated forever. Even if we find ourselves falling away from a pattern, because we originally chose the pattern, we are more likely to recognize the need to reassert our new pattern over the old, because the impetus for the change was originally internal. So, should the patterns begin to revert, we can recognize it and behave accordingly to reorient ourselves on our correct path.

Please note: As part of this Elemental Integration Process, we must actively cultivate all four Elements for our own benefit. This cultivation will bring us out of our comfort zone. If we have gone through our lives only focusing and reacting from the one most-prevalent Element, the influence and characteristics of one of the others might precipitate change, and a sense of discomfort with this new paradigm.

While in the midst of this process, things might begin to feel somewhat chaotic. In part, this is because you are making conscious changes about intimate parts of yourself. It can be daunting to challenge some of these long-held beliefs and modes of behavior. In fact, I would not be surprised if there are times when you wish to stop the process because of discomfort with what is happening. It is at this very point I encourage you to persevere. The instant we are out of our comfort zone, there is a small but insidious part of us that begins to coax us back toward the comfortable and safe, toward the maintenance of the status quo. The second we make a change, decide to keep living that change, and incorporate it into our lives, we will be tempted to cease and desist and go back to what we have known. Should this happen, I urge you to breathe deeply and stay focused on the ultimate goal of truly living your life on your terms.

Your internal voice will guide how you move forward. And since that voice will be your tour guide on this journey, it would be a good thing to get to know that voice. At the end of this chapter is a Meditation on acknowledging this secret part of you. Please take the time to go on that small journey, so you can get a better idea of your own inner wisdom.

Since we have established that no one can truly know another's experience, I state here that this book is not that internal voice. Instead, this book seeks to work in concert with that voice. It reaches out to your secret self. No one else in the world will experience what you experience as you read, work, and play through the many Missions in these pages. You yourself will be "driving the bus" as it were. Anyone and everyone else who picks up this book will have a different experience. Of course the book is here to provide guidance, but you decide the manner in which you undertake the Missions and Meditations. Others who read this book will have different needs, different responses, and different outcomes from each of the Missions. That is as it should be. Since we are all individuals, we not only can, but we should have a unique experience.

The Missions in this book are designed to give you a framework to follow. You might wish to think of this path as a blank canvas. The colors, textures, and composition of each canvas of people who read this book will be entirely different. They will all be canvases, but how they will be created is based strictly on the needs, desires, goals, and wishes of each person.

Meditation "Inner Voice"

Here, please read through the Meditation and then go to http://LifeElements.info. Click the "Meditations" button. Please note: the Meditations page is password protected, since it is intended only for people who are on the Life Elements journey. The password is the word "peace" without the quotes. Once you are at the Meditations page, click the "Inner Voice" mp3 and play it so you may go on the guided journey without distraction.

Lie comfortably on your bed. Once you are comfortable, I want you to focus in on your hands and notice what your fingers are doing. Now, become aware of your forearms and your elbows. Notice what your upper arms are doing and how they are lying. I want you to sense your toes, your ankles, and the backs of your calves, and how they are connected. Notice your hips and your pelvis. Observe your chest and your belly as they expand and contract as you breathe. Feel your belly rise and get fuller as you inhale, and fall and contract as you exhale. Notice your face, your eyes. I want you to try to relax your eyes in your eye sockets. In yoga, they call this "softening your eyes." Try not to concentrate on any one thing with your eyes, and that will help them relax.

Bring your focus down to the shoulder of your dominant hand, and then bring it down to your forearm, and then down to your hand, and to your fingers. I want you to imagine that you are holding a strawberry, a ripe, red strawberry. I want you to see the little seeds on the outside. Notice the strawberry's shape. Turn it over from side to side so you can see the entire thing. When you have it firmly in your mind, let it go.

As you let the strawberry go, in its place, I want you to picture an orange. See if you can picture its slightly puckered skin, and observe its vivid color. When you have it firmly in your mind, let it go.

And now I want you to picture a lemon, a bright yellow lemon. See if you can picture it from all sides. Notice its color and shape. Are there any markings on it? If so, what are they? Once you have the lemon firmly in your mind, let it go.

Now imagine a bright green lime. See how it is a bit smaller than the lemon. Turn it over in your mind and see it from all sides. And when you have it firmly in your mind, let it go. In its place, I want you to imagine a handful of blueberries. See if you can count how many there are, and what they look like. Find the little ruffle at the top of each. Once you have them firmly in your mind, I want you to let them go and I want you to picture a handful of dark indigo, almost black grapes. Notice how the light plays on them. When you have them firmly in your mind, let them go.

Now imagine a bright plum, that violet color that plums can get. And I want you to notice your hand as you hold that plum. Notice your wrist, your forearm, your shoulder and then the rest of your body just as you did before. I want you to notice that you are sitting. You are sitting up and you are holding a plum. And where you are sitting is at a picnic. You have a blanket and some plates, and all of the fruit at which you have been looking is on the plates before you, along with a delicious-looking meal. Notice that you are in a little meadow, and there are wildflowers of many different kinds all around you. Notice that to your left is a little stream. When you originally decided to have a picnic, you decided to put your blanket down by the stream so you could hear it. And it's been merrily babbling away this whole time.

Take a moment here and take pleasure in the healthy and delicious meal before you. Leave the fruit on the plates and allow yourself to savor the tastes and textures as you slowly eat and enjoy your meal. After you have eaten, you decide that you want to take a little walk. You decide to walk and follow the stream for a bit. You get up and you start meandering, just like the stream.

As you walk, you realize that the stream is headed toward a stand of trees up ahead. You decide to keep going, and so you walk into the woods. As you follow the stream through the woods, slowly, you realize the sky is becoming obscured by the trees. It's okay. It feels great; it's just that you notice it as you follow the stream. There's a well-marked path by the stream. And you are able simply to walk along it.

As you walk, you notice there is a fallen oak tree and you walk around it. And then you walk a little bit longer, and you notice there is another fallen tree, and you climb over this one. And as you walk on, you notice that the stream has widened out into a little pond. As you pause by the pond you look around, and you realize that it feels really peaceful to be here. It feels peaceful, and also possessed of a quiet strength. It's familiar to you somehow, and you have a sense of homecoming.

You realize you've been walking for a while, and so maybe it would be good to sit down for a bit and relax. And so you do. You sit down, lean against a tree, and relax by this pond. Allow yourself to soak up the energy of the peace, the strength, the quiet, and the relaxation.

Look into the bottom of the pond. It is so still, you can easily see your reflection. Go ahead and take a look and see what you see. What are the reflections cast by your surroundings? What do you see? As you gaze into the still water, you realize that when you look into the pond, there is a face beside you. It is a face you know from your past. It is gentle and kind, full of strength and wisdom. You realize as you see the face that this being is here to care for you and protect you. This being is with you at all times. It is your inner voice: your internal knowing that comes to you here and now. It is always present to give you wisdom when you take the time to listen, for its interest is always in your highest good.

Honor this being as you honor yourself. Take the time now to acknowledge and give thanks for the inner wisdom that has brought you to this point in time and space. This place, this pond, the trees, sunlight, and earth are here for you to enjoy. Here you can speak with your innermost self and gain conscious wisdom. Now is a time for you to regenerate your sense of peace and strength from this inner guide. Take a few moments and speak to this being. Or if you prefer, just sit silently together.

After you have taken your fill and have had your communion with this being, you realize it is time to head back to your picnic. Thank your inner guide. Look into the pond's cool, clear waters one last time. And then, raise yourself from the comfortable ground. Turn all the way around and look at this place, your place. This is a spot in the universe that is just your own. You can return to it at any time. And in fact, if you wish, all you have to do to return to this peaceful spot is to say the words, "I remember this place," or another phrase you like. Tell yourself you can return to this spot whenever you need a sense of peace, of strength, or simple communion with those who care for you. All you need to do is to say your phrase to yourself, and you will be back in the sheltering arms of the trees and the stillness of the pond.

Now, begin to follow the stream back up the slight incline. Notice the trees that you pass. Step over the fallen tree and then walk around the oak. You begin to notice that the sky overhead is lightening as the leaves are becoming less dense.

As you step out of the stand of trees, notice your surroundings. Has the sky changed? How much time has passed? Has it been only a few minutes, or have you been gone for several hours?

Walk up to your picnic blanket and notice the fruits on the plates. They have been left untouched while you wandered. Sit down on the blanket and relax. Pick up the plum and take a look at it. See its color and notice its shape. And now, put it down and pick up the indigo, almost-black bunch of grapes. After you have taken in their shape and color, put them down and pick up the handful of blueberries. After replacing the blueberries, notice the lime and pick it up. Once you have put it down, pick up the lemon, and then pick up the orange.

Lastly, find the original strawberry you had seen. Feel the strawberry in your hand as you lie down and gently close your eyes while still holding it. Take a deep breath and release the strawberry from your hand. Right now, as you lie here, softly flex the fingers that, in your mind, had held the strawberry. Feel your hand in this time and place. Gently wiggle your fingers, and now, wiggle the ones on the other hand. Slowly allow yourself to come back into your body. Feel your toes and feet, and wiggle your toes. Notice how your legs feel where you are lying. See how your hips and pelvis feel. Notice your stomach and chest, and feel breath come in and out of your body. Awaken your fingers, hands, and arms. And lastly, notice your face, your nose, your mouth, lips, teeth, and tongue, your cheeks, your eyes, your forehead, and the top of your head. Notice that you feel relaxed and rejuvenated, awake and alert.

When you are ready, open your eyes. You have found a place of peace and you have met your inner voice. This is the guide you can follow as you begin the journey to your truest, fullest self.

Chapter 5
Initiate Change

Now we begin the process of you initiating changes on your own behalf. Here we will look at the Elements of Earth, Air, Fire, and Water, and begin this wondrous journey.

In astrology, when a birth chart is done, a person can find out about various personality traits and other factors and issues in his or her life. The Elements that govern the various signs of the zodiac are brought into play to explain behavior patterns and responses. These Elements and descriptions serve a greater purpose. They do a very nice job of categorizing broad personality types, as well as giving rise to the idea that each Element governs a particular type of response to stimuli. For example, a person who is calm and centered will respond quite differently to a given situation than someone who finds himself or herself quick to act. Thus, if we can describe each Element as governing certain personality traits, we can see how these traits interact with one another, both in our relationships with others and more importantly in our relationships with ourselves.

Here are brief descriptions of the Elements.

Earth is centeredness and stability. The earth is solid under our feet and we depend on it to remain so.

Air is thought and reason. Air is clear, and through it we can see the truth.

Fire is motion, creation, passion, and destruction. Fire and heat are used to create many things, yet to create something fire must also destroy its medium, such as wood or other materials.

Water is fluid and ever changing, just like our emotions and our intuition. One of my favorite phrases that describes someone's emotional state is: Still waters run deep.

Following these symbolic interpretations, our general personalities and reactions to new stimuli can be delineated in the same manner. When we study a new situation or challenge, we can begin to see how we might approach it while using the Elements.

Here is a possible order of responses, both internal and external, when a person is faced with a new challenge. First, we receive the challenge while in a centered place [Earth]. Then we perceive what we feel, feel it, and acknowledge our feelings [Water]. Next, we think through the situation and develop a plan of action [Air], and then use our strengths and passions to act [Fire].

If you are characterized by one Element, then that Element will play the most significant role in your response to situations. In cases where your Element is the one that yields the most appropriate response, you will reap the greatest benefit. However, the question must be raised about situations when your strongest Element is not the most appropriate. What then? What else can we draw upon to help us respond appropriately to situations that arise in our lives? I believe that we need to strengthen our bonds with *all* of the Elements to be able to access the strengths and characteristics of each one. Then, we will be able to give the most appropriate response to whatever situations arise.

This book proposes that when and where you are born does not necessarily dictate your personality traits and influencing Elements. Rather, your personality traits and tendencies indicate what Element most closely aligns with you. For example, someone who was born in October, and is an Air sign, Libra, might not have many of the traditional Libra characteristics of balancing, trouble with decision-making, and an inclination toward peacemaking. In fact, she or he might have quite a passionate and fiery personality. She might leap before she looks, act first and ask questions later. Therefore, when she identifies an association with one or another Element, she might decide that she is much more a Fire personality than an Air personality. This decision is part of the assessment we must all complete to determine our current Elemental status.

While only the first step on the road to personal fulfillment, this assessment of our present status is crucial to the beginning of the Integration Process. The EDAT and EIAT are your tools for making that determination. Once you have your Element Designation, you are free to move forward to the next steps of integration. I assert that it is both possible and necessary to cultivate the characteristics of all of the Elements to become truly well-rounded beings. If we find ourselves influenced by one Element over the others, we will want to cultivate the other Elements to augment our skill set in dealing with both everyday and life-path issues. Or, if we find ourselves lacking in the influence of one Element in particular, we will wish to cultivate its strength as our own. Conversely, if we find we are too strong in one Element or another, we might want to decrease our dependence on and connection to that Element. Put in simple terms, first, we figure out where we currently sit. Then, we figure out where to go from there.

People who are strong in only one Element tend to have one main way of looking at and reacting to the world. So, for example, an Air person might approach most if not all situations from the perspective of reason, logic, and thought. That method is not only comfortable, but is often at least somewhat effective in handling the hills and valleys of the life path. The challenge with being strong in only one Element occurs when a situation arises that requires a different skill set to deal with it effectively. So, let us take a look at an example of when the Air Element's sphere of influence of reason and logic might not be the best way to resolve an issue.

Imagine the following scenario. Mark is an Air Element Designation. He tends to resolve issues by thinking them through and developing a methodical, logical approach for overcoming obstacles. He has recently begun dating a woman who is very much a Water Element person. Delia is the type of person who reacts immediately from her emotions. She feels things deeply, and is always interested in discussing and expressing how she feels. At one point, she complains to Mark that her boss is making her upset. He has once again taken credit for her work, and she is hurt and more than a little angry. Mark reacts from an Air Element perspective and immediately begins to think up plans and potential solutions to speak to the boss and to resolve the situation. He presents them to Delia in a logical fashion, because as an Air person, that is exactly the kind of help he would wish to receive if he found himself in a similar situation. He would want to hear how he might approach the boss, what he might say, an itemized list of concerns, and possible resolutions.

However, Delia, as an emotion-centered Water personality, needs to receive an emotion-perspective response. Rather than immediately beginning to think up resolutions, she is initially interested in having her partner comfort her and soothe her wounded feelings. When she tells Mark she is hurt, and that he is not understanding her, that she is not interested in discussing how to fix it and what plans to make, he in turn is mystified, because he was simply trying to help her in the way he knew best.

If Mark had stronger affinity to Water, he might have intuitively heard and understood that Delia's need for comfort came before her need to resolve the issue with her boss. On the other hand, if Delia had stronger Air characteristics in addition to her Water influences, she might have been able to acknowledge her feelings and then mitigate them by making room to think through possible solutions. She would have been able to enter into a more reasoned-out, problem-solver mode as well, and might likely have reacted quite differently to Mark's attempts to develop a plan of action. At this point, however, she was more interested in the Water qualities of Mark hearing her sadness and acknowledging her emotions than she was in the more Air activity of how to resolve the situation and confront her supervisor.

Sometimes, these kinds of miscommunications can create issues between people, and yet they only occur because those people are approaching a given situation from two different perspectives. It is possible that if Mark had been able to access his emotional Water characteristics, he might have been able to provide the emotional connection and comfort Delia needed. It is also possible that if Delia had a stronger association with Air, she might have been in a much better place to hear and develop a plan of action on how to handle and resolve the issue between her and her boss.

Here is an example where the Elemental energies might be complementary, and where cultivation of new Elements can develop. James, an Earth personality, is distraught about some weight he has gained. He tends to be a homebody, and spends a good bit of time at his computer. Marcia is a Fire personality, and is always on the go. When James expresses his distraught state about his weight gain, Marcia responds that he might want to get out and start exercising more. In fact, she suggests they take up walking together as a way to get them both out and moving. Note that her response does not leave James to begin his exercise regimen alone. She was willing and motivated to get involved and do something to help him. This helps give James impetus to begin to move, and provides support in an active manner.

If James had more access to Fire characteristics to begin with, he might have motivated himself to start an exercise regimen. As it is, he gets motivation from his friend's Fire characteristics. This, in turn, will give him greater access to the "in-motion" influence of Fire, and will give him greater access to Fire later.

The more we develop our accessibility to the Elements and the easier it becomes to access each one when we need it, the easier we will move through our life path. Sometimes this access occurs organically, as in the case of James and Marcia. Sometimes it must be actively cultivated, which would have benefitted Mark and Delia in their exchange.

If we need an emotional connection or an intuitive response, then the Water Element's characteristics are needed. If a situation calls for a more reasoned approach, then Air is the Element to which to turn. Fire will bring active motion; Earth will bring stability. It all depends on which is needed at the time. Thus, as you take the EDAT, regardless of which Element or Elements come up as your strongest influences, you will eventually want to increase and then balance your connections with all four Elements. You will use many of the Missions and Meditations later in the book to balance your Elemental characteristics, and then you will have access to each when each is needed.

When all four Elements are in balance, we can approach our lives from a place of connection and centeredness, and can call upon the characteristics of whichever Element is appropriate for the situation. For example, if we need decisive action, then we can look to the forward motion and passionate energy of Fire to guide us. If the situation calls for thoughtful decision-making, Air's reason and steadfast thinking will be of great help. The rest of this book will show you how both to assess where you currently reside and how to work with the Elements to increase your own access to their governing characteristics. Through the Missions and Meditations, you will imbue yourself with Elemental characteristics and integrate them into your instinctive responses and personality traits.

It is possible to say we are the sum of all of our responses to what has been presented to us in our lives. For example, if we are having an argument with a parent or other loved one, we can either respond as we normally might by yelling or reacting quickly (Fire influence), or by crying (Water influence). Or, we might change our approach and step back to delve into what is underneath the issue. If we center ourselves (Earth influence), we can approach the interaction from a calm, centered place. From this calm place, we might think through to a solution (Air influence). At the least, we will be free to listen and feel our emotions, to assess them without judgment, and simultaneously extend the same courtesy to the person with whom we are speaking. Then, we might just change the outcome of what could have been a big argument.

There are other examples we might study. How might the Elements be used to approach the end of a relationship, rearing children, addressing a concern at work, or moving forward in your career? Each of these scenarios can be addressed through the Elements: the stability of Earth, the mindfulness of Air, the creativity of Fire and the compassion of Water. Eventually we will want to be strong in all of them, but first we must assess which one(s) currently guide us.

This book utilizes two main tools for determining which Element guides your personality. The Element Designation Assessment and the Element Imbalance Assessment Tools assess your Element Designation and identify any potential Element Imbalances. Once you have evaluated your current Designation through the EDAT and EIAT, you will be directed to proceed on one of two tracks to Integration. If you have no Imbalances, you will proceed to track one and cultivate the Elements through the Element Designation chapters. If you do have any Imbalances, you will need to proceed to track two by addressing any Imbalances through the Element Imbalance chapters. Both tracks will teach you more about your Element status and then help you balance Element strength, distribution, and enhancement. At the end of each Element Designation, Imbalance, and Combination chapter, there is a road map to continue the Integration Process. The Missions and Meditations included in the book will then help you strengthen your connection to each, to create a balance of all of them.

I believe, quite strongly, that we have a deep knowledge of what is best for us, and that you already possess the strength to make the changes you want and need in your life even if you have not yet accessed it. As you work through the Missions and Meditations, you will begin to notice you have new access to ideas and behavior patterns, ones different from those with which you are familiar. For example, once you have worked through the exercises to strengthen the Earth Element, you will likely find that you have a more solid foundation and your sense of stability has increased. When those two things occur, you can then incorporate those aspects of the Earth Element and use them in your daily life. When you have completed all the appropriate Missions, you will have quick access to each of the Elements. You will then be able to move forward, secure in the knowledge that you have the ability to approach any situation in a well-rounded and even peaceful state. With the strength and connection of each Element comes an enduring peace and contentment.

Ideally, we want to draw upon the properties of each Element when it is needed. As an example, if you have a sticky office issue to navigate, you might need the reasoning of Air, the perceptiveness of Water, the certainty and stability of Earth, and Fire's motion when it is time to act and resolve the problem. However, someone who is not strong in Fire might see the issue, know how to resolve it, and see who needs guidance (or be able to perceive exactly how everyone feels and therefore the best way to proceed in communication with those involved), but might be unable either to calm the situation or initiate the necessary actions to resolve the issue. Or, they will not act when the opportunity presents itself. Conversely, a person who is too strong in Fire might seize an opportunity without having thought of the potential consequences.

Put in basic terms, if the person is lucky, then quick action might work out well. If they are not lucky, well, then, the quick action might turn out to have been rash. As a review, here are the steps you will need to take to best use this book for achieving balance and self-actualization.

1. Honor yourself for starting this to begin with, since it can be frightening to take the reins. I am perfectly serious in this statement. Many people do courageous things every day, and they do not take the time to honor that they have done them. Sometimes just doing that, just taking the first step, is the most important part. So, please take the time to do something good for yourself. Put the book down and sit quietly and acknowledge the courage and perseverance that have brought you to this point. No doubt it can be frightening to decide to make changes in our lives and then move forward to make those changes. Since you have begun this process, it is only fitting to earmark it with some kind of ceremony. You might wish to light a candle. You might wish to go for a walk. Or, you might simply wish to sit and gently breathe while you take time to honor your intent to make a difference: to make a change that will move you forward more authentically and happily.

2. Determine where you are right now by completing the assessments (both the EDAT and eventually the EIAT). To complete the tasks in this book, you must first know where you are starting.

3. Once you have taken the EDAT, you will have learned your Element Designation(s). At this point, it is beneficial to once again honor where you currently stand. If you are strong in one Element, please do the Meditation to honor that Element, because its influence, at least in part, has gotten you to this point. Your reliance on the reason of Air, the intuition of Water, the motion of Fire, or the stability of Earth have helped you survive and perhaps even thrive until now, so it is important to accept where you have been and to pay tribute to that which has gotten you this far.

4. Next, it is important to identify any Elemental Imbalances. To do this, you will need to complete the EIAT. If you find you have an Imbalance in an Element, you can begin the process of balancing your Imbalances.

For example, if you have a Water Imbalance, that likely means you find yourself more emotional, moody, and sensitive than you are comfortable with, and you might wish to change that aspect of yourself. The best way to do that is to find a calm, reasoned place inside yourself where you can think through what is happening to you rather than simply reacting emotionally. An emotional reaction likely leaves you feeling drained and unhappy, and then it is much more challenging to experience your true feelings. When you attempt to experience your emotions and resolve any issues, the pain might be too great, and you might find yourself unwilling to delve deeply enough to achieve resolution.

If you can instead find that calm center and think through what has happened and what makes you feel the way you do, you might achieve a sense of reason behind what happened and what gave rise to your emotions. So, the best way to handle a Water Imbalance is to increase the Air Element influence in your day-to-day actions and experiences. This will occur regardless of which Imbalances are revealed. You will mitigate your Imbalances until none exists, and then you will be ready for the final step.

5. Finally, you will cultivate the Elements you were not exhibiting by following the prescribed guidelines at the end of each Element Designation description chapter. Once you have completed all of them, you will be ready to honor your completion of the Integration Process. Please note: this process does not occur immediately, and it might take a few times through the Missions before you begin to see the Element working in your life. Keep at it. You will be surprised at how much will open up for you.

Chapter 6
Element Designation Introduction and Assessment Tool

Assessment questions will help to determine which of the Elements has the most governance over the manner in which you live. In addition, you will also use the EIAT assessment questions to determine if you have any Elemental Imbalance. Just as we can be strong in an Element, we can also have too much (or too little) affinity with it and therefore have an Elemental Imbalance. Since we are dynamic beings, our strengths and personalities ebb and flow over time. This means our access to and reliance on the potency of the Elements and our states of thinking, feeling, acting, and being will change over time. However, since we are focusing on the present, we need to find exactly where we sit to know how to proceed. As such, I have developed the Element Designation Assessment Tool.

This assessment is a series of questions you will need to think about and answer. I say "think about" because often when we take these types of assessments, we answer too quickly and without sufficient thought. The EDAT is strictly to help you find your current state—where you sit in your own mind and heart. Thus, no one will ever see it unless you choose to reveal it. I encourage you to be as honest as you can, and to know this is strictly to help you follow your true path. The EDAT will determine your Element Designation. This means it will help you name which Element or Elements currently play a major role in the manner in which you view and act in the world. Since these Elements describe an affinity with one of four states—thinking, feeling, acting, and being—their influences can also describe and even predict the manner in which we will behave or react to various situations. The EDAT helps ascertain this information. Once you know which Element(s) describe or have governance over you, you can then follow the various steps in the book to integrate the rest.

Please note, the EDAT is available online. You might take the EDAT online, and then go from there directly back to the book to continue the Integration Process. To access the online version of the EDAT, go to http://LifeElements.info, click the "Assessments" button, and then click the Element Designation Assessment Tool (EDAT) link.

If you will complete the assessment in the book, please check the white check box in the corresponding row to the right of the statement for each statement generally true for you. Once you have completed this section, you will add your score vertically down the columns by counting the number of boxes you checked in each column. In other words, you will add all the boxes you checked in Column A and tabulate the score at the bottom of the Table, and then you will add the boxes you checked in Column B, and then Column C, and so forth. The largest number of the four columns is your score, and it will give you your Element Designation.

Once you know which of those columns (A, B, C, or D) gave you the greatest number of true statements, look at the corresponding set of instructions detailing where to read your Element Designation. Please read the Element description and review whether the description appears to be true for you.

There is no time limit for this assessment tool. Simply select the box on the same row for every statement that is generally true for you.

Element Designation Assessment Tool

EDAT Questions	A	B	C	D
1. I am a romantic person.	■			☐
2. I tend to spend a lot of time analyzing situations that have occurred.	■	☐		
3. I am goal-oriented.	■		☐	

EDAT Questions	A	B	C	D
4. Listening to music can easily change my mood.				☐
5. I believe sex is most wonderful when the partners are in love.				☐
6. I strive to have my home be clean and tidy.	☐			
7. I keep in close contact with friends.	☐			
8. People have told me that I am a very good listener.		☐		
9. I am able to keep a calm head in a crisis.		☐		
10. I believe intimacy is the most important part of sex.				☐
11. I tend to be the first person to react to an unexpected occurrence.			☐	
12. I keep in close contact with my family.	☐			
13. I tend to be the person my friends seek out when they are going through a rough time.				☐
14. I work very hard to achieve my goals.			☐	
15. I tend to spend a lot of time replaying and analyzing conversations.		☐		
16. I have a lot of energy.			☐	
17. My ideal career would be in a field where I can help people, particularly as a counselor or therapist of some sort.				☐
18. I believe trust is the most important part of sex.	☐			
19. I have an easy and comfortable relationship with most of my friends.	☐			
20. If I were an artist, I would be a performing artist such as an actor, comedian, or some other type of performer.			☐	
21. I thrive on deadlines.			☐	

EDAT Questions	A	B	C	D
22. When presented with a problem, my first impulse is to look at and think through every facet of the situation before I make any moves.		☐		
23. I am hardly ever jealous or envious.				☐
24. I tend to take on many responsibilities, and I live up to them for the most part.	☐			
25. I can sense how other people are feeling, and I can tell what will help them feel better.				☐
26. My favorite creative outlet is writing, and I might have a journal in which I keep my private thoughts and creative writing.		☐		
27. When I need to assemble something such as furniture, I simply begin the work because I believe the procedure will become clear as I go along.			☐	
28. I am an overachiever.			☐	
29. I believe a sense of security is the most important part of a relationship.	☐			
30. I consider myself to have a very passionate nature.			☐	
31. I enjoy thinking through to the solutions to problems.			☐	
32. I love to be surprised.			☐	
33. My favorite creative outlet is music, and I do or have played an instrument or sung.				☐
34. I believe good communication is the most important part of any relationship.			☐	
35. Sometimes it takes me a while to connect with people, but once I do make the connection, it can be a lifelong one.				☐
36. I respect and follow my intuition.				☐
37. I am genuinely pleased at other people's successes.				☐

EDAT Questions	A	B	C	D
38. People have told me I am a very sensible person.	☑			
39. I believe good communication is the most important part of sex.		☑		
40. Having a stable job/career is very important to me.	☑			
41. I am generally able to forgive people who have hurt my feelings.				☑
42. My life revolves around those with whom I am close.				☑
43. I am not very concerned with how other people see me.	☑			
44. I find I am the support system to most people I know.	☑			
45. I am most comfortable with a written schedule or to-do list.		☑		
46. When I encounter an issue in my relationship, I immediately begin to think of ways to resolve it.		☑		
47. I am fond of trying new foods and enjoy many and varied cuisines.			☑	
48. I would describe myself as a softhearted person.				☑
49. I enjoy working with my hands and doing crafts like knitting or woodworking.	☑			
50. People see me as a pretty spontaneous person.			☑	
51. I work best when I can pace myself. That way, I am assured of a good quality finished product.	☑			
52. I believe passion is the most important part of sex.			☑	
53. I thrive on challenges both at work and at home.			☑	

EDAT Questions	A	B	C	D
54. Most people see me as a shoulder to lean on in times of trouble.	■			
55. I often act as the calming force in my circle of friends.		■		
56. When presented with a problem, my first impulse is to do something to solve it.			■	
57. When I need to assemble something such as furniture, I read the directions and then begin at the beginning.		■		
58. I enjoy my material possessions.	■			
59. I tend to complete projects on time.	■			
60. I am at my happiest when I make someone else happy.				■
61. Generally, at parties, I tend to be the first one on the dance floor.			■	
62. I am practical.	■			
63. I enjoy my physical body and all its many capabilities.	■			
64. I enjoy figuring out how things work.		■		
65. When I need to assemble something such as furniture, I envision how everything needs to fit and follow my instincts to complete the project.				■
66. I prefer to have solid plans in place for any situation, and I can become uncomfortable if plans change suddenly.		■		
67. I am a kind and sympathetic person.				■
68. I communicate well and honestly with friends and family.		■		
69. Sometimes, a comfortable chair and a good book make for a wonderful Saturday night.	■			
70. I trust my reason rather than my feelings.		■		
71. I meditate.	■			
72. I thoroughly enjoy meeting new people.			■	

EDAT Questions	A	B	C	D
73. When presented with a problem, my first impulse is to develop a plan of action.		☐		
74. I enjoy the excitement of being spontaneous.			☐	
75. I enjoy working with others in the spirit of cooperation.				☐
76. I believe I have honest and stable relationships with people.	☐			
77. I tend to make quick emotional connections with people.				☐
78. I tend to have a lot of ideas for new things to do and to try.			☐	
79. I want to plan out activities.		☐		
80. If I were an artist, I would paint, and when I look at art, I find myself drawn to the flow and use of shape and color.				☐
81. If I were an artist, I would do sculpture or ceramics, and I have always enjoyed the texture or tangibility of art.	☐			
82. I find it easy to express my true feelings.				☐
83. I enjoy intellectually challenging, in-depth conversations.		☐		
84. I love competition.			☐	
85. When presented with a problem, my first impulse is to think through all possible solutions.		☐		
86. I get bored quite easily.			☐	
87. If I were an artist, I would draw, especially with pen or pencil. When I look at art, I find myself drawn to the use of line and contrast.		☐		
88. I prefer serious discussions to loud, boisterous, on-the-surface conversations.		☐		
89. People have told me that talking to me about a problem often helps them feel better.				☐

EDAT Questions	A	B	C	D
90. I view getting lost as an opportunity to explore.			☐	
91. I enjoy rapid-fire banter and quick, witty conversation.			☐	
92. I trust my feelings rather than my reason.				☐
93. I am a self-starter and am self-motivated, especially about projects I find interesting.			☐	
94. I like making sure everything has a place and things are neatly stored away.	☐			
95. I jump right into new projects.			☐	
96. I generally feel comfortable in new environments.	☐			
97. I find new and unusual situations exciting, and I am adventurous.			☐	
98. I want my life to be filled with intellectual challenges.		☐		
99. I tend to be affected strongly by other people's troubles.				☐
100. I am most comfortable with accomplishing tasks on my own time.	☐			

If you have completed the EDAT in the book, it is time to add the check boxes vertically down their respective columns. Add all the check marks you made in Column A and enter them in the appropriate space below. Do the same for each of the other columns. **Your current Element Designation is the column with the greatest number**. You might have more than one column that yields a high number. If you have two or more sections that yield scores higher than 17, then you can categorize yourself as a combination of multiple Elements. The Descriptions that follow the EDAT address both single Element Designation and then later multiple-Element Combinations.

Totals for Column A: _____ B: _____ C: _____ D: _____

Now that you know your Element Designation letter, you need to find the corresponding Element description and characteristics.

The Element Designation for Column A is **Earth**. If your highest result was for Column A, then Earth is your ED. Please turn to that section on page 57 to read the Description and characteristics. These should describe your general state of being and the current manner in which you approach many situations in your life.

The Element Designation for Column B is **Air**. If your highest result was for Column B, then Air is your ED. Please turn to that section on page 59 to read the Description and characteristics. These should describe your general state of being and the current manner in which you approach many situations in your life.

The Element Designation for Column C is **Fire**. If your highest result was for Column C, then Fire is your ED. Please turn to that section on page 60 to read the Description and characteristics. These should describe your general state of being and the current manner in which you approach many situations in your life.

The Element Designation for Column D is **Water**. If your highest result was for Column D, then Water is your ED. Please turn to that section on page 62 to read the Description and characteristics. These should describe your general state of being and the current manner in which you approach many situations in your life.

The Descriptions will characterize your trends and tendencies. They are general descriptions of personality types and our states of thinking, feeling, acting, and being. Please note that no one person is all one Element. We all have an amalgam of the Elements present at any one time. However, often, one Element is the dominant force in our actions, reactions, and states of being. As such, it is possible that certain parts of the Descriptions might not feel pertinent. The important thing to remember here is that we are seeking a starting place from which to begin this Integration Process. We will learn and know how to cultivate the Elements, and how to increase or decrease our connection to and reliance on any one Element, so we then have access to all four when situations call for the beneficial influence of one or another.

Please note: if you received a score of over 17 for more than one Element, then you are a combination of Elements. If this has occurred for you, please do read the Element Designation Description(s) below for the individual Elements. Then, read the chapter titled Element Combinations (starting on page 65), because a combination of Elements yields a special set of influences and must be addressed additionally.

Please do read the Element Designation Description(s) following. However, once you have read them, you will want to stop before the "How Do You Proceed?" section and take the Element Imbalance Assessment Test (EIAT). You will follow one of the two tracks, depending on your Element Imbalance status. If you find you have any Elemental Imbalances, you will want to address them and then follow the track to the Integration Process from that point. Both tracks will take you on your journey to a whole and balanced life; the second track will help you alleviate any Imbalances before you continue the process.

Chapter 7
Element Designation Descriptions

Column A: Earth Element Designation
You are a stable, practical individual. You are serious and matter-of-fact and you believe it is most important to live in a secure environment. You are most concerned with the material of life. You attempt to resolve issues from a solid, calm approach. You are often generous and unselfish. You have a very sensible approach to life and you have few, if any, pretensions. However, sometimes you are so stable, it can be difficult to move you from your chosen perch. You are certain of yourself and where you are in life.

You tend to be a homebody, and you enjoy the quiet times. There are times when you are too much of a homebody and you currently have few adventures, but you appear to be generally okay with that. You are concerned with your physical body, and you might currently be undergoing a period of motivation to improve your health. It would not be surprising to find you are currently practicing or thinking about starting yoga, Tai Chi or one of the other internal disciplines. These will allow you to maintain health and vitality without the need for competition or rivalry. You find yourself the solid, centered confidant of those who tend to flit around you and often need your stable presence to help ground them.

You tend to trust your senses and you need to have things shown or proven to you before you will believe them. Trust is the most important aspect of your relationships and stability does not lag too far behind.

You evaluate and judge all of the things that come across your path from a pragmatic standpoint. You are not particularly a risk-taker, and that seems to be just fine for you. Right now, you do not appear to be interested in struggling to achieve. You appear to be in a more settled place in your life.

You are likely handy, and you are able fix most things that need fixing. You like to work with your hands, and you very much dwell in the material world of the senses.

Because you are centered, you nurture and encourage the success of others. People come to you when they need steady, practical advice and a calm sounding board.

There are times when you can be too settled and sedentary. You will watch too much television or play on the computer late into the night. You get into what might be called ruts, and have a challenging time of breaking out of them. There are also times when your practical nature can run counter to some of the other things you might want to do, and you end up "playing it safe" rather than reaching for what you really want.

How Do You Proceed?

Please note: Before you go any further, read Chapter 9 and take the EIAT, and address any Element Imbalances. If you take the EIAT and have no Imbalances, come back to this point in the book and continue forward. If you do have any Imbalances, you will continue the Integration Process from the point at which you alleviate your Imbalances.

At this point, you have a solid foundation from which to start the next part of the Integration Process. You already possess the stable center, and it is a good idea to honor that which you already exhibit, so please complete the "Guided Meditation to the Earth Element" in Chapter 13.

Once you have acknowledged your current status, continue to access and integrate the rest of the Elements. We will begin with the thought process that moves so fluidly out of a quiet, stable center. Please go to Chapter 15 on Air Missions and Meditations and complete them. Afterward, you will move on to cultivate your emotional heart center with the Water Missions and Meditations

(Chapter 18). Then, you will access Fire's passion and forward motion (Chapter 17). Once you have completed all of the Missions and Meditations, please go to Chapters 19 and 20 and conclude the Integration Process.

Column B: Air Element Designation

You are analytical and thought-oriented. You have a facile mind and you tend to be quick witted. You prefer to reason your way through life. You love in-depth communication and you value analysis. You enjoy following things step by step to their conclusion. You can be stubborn once you have reached an opinion or decision. After you have given an issue some thought, very little will sway you. You are gifted with seeing the myriad facets of any situation. You are able to think your way through most issues. However, that might keep you from truly experiencing them because you are so busy analyzing them even as you live through them. You value your mind and its abilities. You look at the world through the eyes of reason and logic. And you live best in the world of ideas.

You tend to have good language skills, and you make convincing arguments. You are analytical and tend to be good at games and other such challenges. You tend to give well-thought-out advice and arguments, and you relish a good debate.

There are times when you can over think things in your quest to reach the right decision, and it can be quite challenging for you actually to reach a decision. Even when you know the best course of action, your analytical nature can make it challenging for you to act. There are also times when your analytical nature makes it seem as if you are disconnected from your feelings. In fact, there are times when you are able to disconnect from what you feel and become quite dispassionate when the feelings you might experience are too painful. Some have described this as "shutting down."

Truth and honesty are of utmost importance to you, and once someone has lied to you, it can take you a long time to trust again. You will face the truth regardless of the consequences. You tend to play by the rules and want everyone to follow them well. You are straightforward and forthright with those around you, and you rebel against deception.

How Do You Proceed?

Please note: Before you go any further, read Chapter 9 and take the EIAT, and address any Element Imbalances. If you take the EIAT and have no Imbalances, come back to this point in the book and continue forward. If you do have any Imbalances, you will continue the Integration Process from the point at which you alleviate your Imbalances. At this point, you have a foundation of reason and thought from which to start the next part of the Integration Process.

Since you already possess the clarity necessary to complete the rest of the process, it is a good idea to honor that which you already exhibit. So, please complete the "Guided Meditation to the Air Element" in Chapter 13. Once you have acknowledged your current status, continue to access and integrate the rest of the Elements. We will begin to cultivate your energy and passion to act and achieve with Fire Missions and Meditations. (Please complete the Missions and Meditations in Chapter 17.) Then, we will move to developing the stable foundation and center of Earth (Chapter 16). After this, you will access your emotional heart center with the Water Missions and Meditations (Chapter 18).

Once you have completed all the Missions and Meditations, go to Chapters 19 and 20 to conclude the Integration Process.

Column C: Fire Element Designation

You are a passionate and fiery individual. You tend to be dynamic and always on the go. You are outgoing and charismatic, and the people in your life see you as very enthusiastic. You have an active life and you seldom sit still for long. You might love to play sports or dance, and you have a readily apparent vitality.

You are positive and optimistic. You are constantly being inspired with new ideas, and always have many plans of action in motion at any one time. You believe anything is possible, and will work to ensure that your dreams come true. You are also optimistic and supportive of the dreams of those around you. One of your favorite pastimes might be to brainstorm on new adventures or ideas to make life even more fun. You want your life to be an adventure, and are willing to do what is necessary to have it be so. You have a bright outlook and are not easily discouraged.

You tend to stay busy constantly, and are never satisfied with the status quo. As soon as you accomplish one goal, you are off to begin the next big adventure.

Passion and excitement tend to be of utmost importance to you in a relationship, and you can be hard pressed to maintain relationships that do not keep both of those alive.

You are innovative, and you can develop ideas into projects and projects into success.

Some might describe you as a dominant or dynamic personality. You are a natural leader and inspire others with your own brand of charm and enthusiasm.

You confront challenges head on.

There are times when you find yourself stretched too thin and too scattered. You move so quickly from one interest to the next, you might not be able to spend solid time on any of them. And then you might begin to feel nothing is getting the attention it deserves. You might also feel like you cannot stop the merry-go-round to give things the attention they need. Last, you might find your dynamic and charismatic nature can get in the way of what you really want to accomplish.

How Do You Proceed?

Please note: Before you go any further, read Chapter 9 and take the EIAT, and address any Element Imbalances. If you take the EIAT and have no Imbalances, come back to this point in the book and continue forward. If you do have any Imbalances, you will continue the Integration Process from the point at which you alleviate your Imbalances.

At this point, you have a foundation of energy and action from which to start the next part of the Integration Process. Since you already possess the energy necessary to complete the rest of the process, it is a good idea to honor that which you already exhibit. So, please complete the "Guided Meditation to the Fire Element" in Chapter 13. Once you acknowledge your current status, continue to access and integrate the rest of the Elements.

We will begin by cultivating Air's thoughtfulness and clarity so you act with more deliberation. (Please complete the

Missions and Meditations in Chapter 15.) Next, we will access your emotional heart center with the Water Missions and Meditations (Chapter 18). Then, you will build the stable foundation and center of Earth (Chapter 16). Once you have completed all the Missions and Meditations, please go to Chapters 19 and 20 and conclude the Integration Process.

Column D: Water Element Designation

You tend to view the world from an intuitive, compassionate perspective. You react to situations from an emotional place, and you express your feelings when the need arises. Many would call you softhearted, and a very sympathetic person. You are always willing to help those in need, even when it is sometimes counter to your own needs. You tend to be extremely loving and caring of those around you. You are moved by the pain and troubles of others. You are often the one people seek to help them through troubled times. Kindness is one of the most important aspects of life to you, as is generosity of spirit. You possess a great deal of intuitive ability, and you can trust your intuition to guide you in the right direction. You tend to follow your gut feelings, and allow your heart rather than your head to guide you in decisions. You tend to have a truly compassionate nature. Because you understand what others are feeling, you find yourself more patient than you might otherwise be.

Water people tend to be conceptual thinkers. You tend to imagine the solutions to problems. You see the resolution all at once rather than in a step-by-step fashion.

Peace and harmony among those around you tend to be very important to you. People come to you for advice, in part because you are well versed in human nature. You are also diplomatic and tactful. You exhibit wisdom beyond your years. You value beauty in all its forms, and you seek inner wisdom.

You do not need to bend others to your will, because you can relate to people on the deepest levels and see you are connected on the heart/love plane. Others can relate to you and trust you because your kindness outshines almost any other part of you.

Love and kindness tend to be the most important aspect of a relationship to you.

There are times when your emotional nature can overwhelm you, and you find yourself sensitive to the slightest issues. At times like these, you can become wrapped up in issues to the point you have trouble articulating your position. You might find yourself simply reacting to what occurs rather than being able to accept and express your feelings and proceed to resolve the issues. At such times, the only thing you can do is to be upset. Your moods can swing, and once hurt, it can take you a while to get back on even ground.

How Do You Proceed?

Please note: Before you go any further, read Chapter 9 and take the EIAT, and address any Element Imbalances. If you take the EIAT and have no Imbalances, come back to this point in the book and continue forward. If you do have any Imbalances, you will continue the Integration Process from the point at which you alleviate your Imbalances.

At this point, you have a foundation of emotional awareness and compassion from which to start the next part of the Integration Process. Since you already possess the awareness necessary to complete the rest of the process, it is a good idea to honor that which you already exhibit. So, please complete the "Guided Meditation to the Water Element" in Chapter 13.

Once you have acknowledged your current status, you will continue to access and integrate the rest of the Elements. We will begin to cultivate your energy and passion to act and achieve with Fire Missions and Meditations. (Please complete the Missions and Meditations in Chapter 17.) Next, we will move to developing the stable foundation and center of Earth (Chapter 16). Then, you will access Air's thoughtfulness and clarity (Chapter 15). Once you have completed all of the Missions and Meditations, please go to Chapters 19 and 20 and conclude the Integration Process.

Chapter 8
Element Combination Descriptions

The EDAT tells us much in the way of information about ourselves. From it, we learn some of our tendencies, patterns of behavior, and instinctive responses. Although the highest score yields which Element most influences our instinctive patterns, some of us might find we already have characteristics of more than one Element. If you found this is the case for you, please read the Element Designations for each individual Element first so you can familiarize yourself with those characteristics. Then, return here to continue to look at your Elemental Combination. You will then proceed on the Integration Process from this point.

First, let me say you are already on your way to becoming fully well rounded, simply because you are strong in multiple Elements. However, just like when cleaning a room, you have probably noticed it looks more scattered while in the process of cleaning than before you started. The same thing can occur here. When you are guided primarily by one Element and its characteristics, things can seem like they are moving forward even if they are not coming from the fully integrated place we have been discussing. While the fully integrated place develops from a balance of all four Elements, the strength and characteristics of one Element have stood many in good stead for millennia. Now, we find ourselves on the precipice of a new way of being, and all four Elements become increasingly important. With characteristics of one Element being dominant, you have one path to follow in your interactions with the world around you. There is always some consistent method of moving forward, whether it is through emotions, actions, thoughts, or the simple state of being.

However, things get a bit shaken up when we have the characteristics of more than one Element playing a role in our lives.

Once you have strength in more than one Element, you will notice there can be a push-pull effect coming to play. For example, if you are a Fire personality, there might have been plenty of times when you leaped before you looked, as they say. However, there likely have not been many times that you spent agonizing over the decisions you made. To an extent, a Fire person makes decisions quickly, acts on them, and then moves on. However, if there is a new Air influence to the already-present Fire, then the thinking-oriented portion becomes both a blessing and a hindrance. The Air now gives voice to the thoughts about actions that have been or are about to be taken. Now, there are more things to handle, and it can become challenging to do so when you are being guided: in effect, pulled into sometimes polar opposite directions.

This push-pull brings an entirely new dimension to Life Elements. Now, we find ourselves in the position of being guided from multiple corners and viewpoints, and we must navigate these waters carefully. Each Element will vie for influence as we live, make our decisions, and move forward. We will become masters of our own lives as we begin to take control of which Elemental parts of ourselves will hold sway over how we live.

Multiple Elements can create less-than-stable situations, because we become uncertain how to act or react when pulled in numerous directions. If we have always been multiple Elements, we might have always lived with the pull of two or more different ways to be. The key here is not to be sidetracked by the pull of each Element, but to become aware of how each can help you move forward. Each Elemental influence does have a process for moving forward. We must draw strength and awareness from each of the Elemental tools in our toolbox, because one or more might be appropriate at any time. With the knowledge that each has characteristics that can be helpful, we will be able to decide how best to proceed. If you have a Combination, you will have multiple Elemental strengths on which to draw. After all, the entire focal point of this process is to develop all four Elements. So, if you already have strength in more than one, you are, as they say, ahead of the game.

If, once you have taken the EDAT, you find you already have Designations in more than one Element, you might find some of these paths are easier to forge. For example, if you are an Air/Earth person, you might find it easier to maintain your sense of peace and center, and all the while think through to solutions for problems than someone who is simply designated as an Air person. Conversely, a Fire/Air person might quickly think through to potential solutions and jump in right away, rather than wait until the time is right to begin work to resolve the issues at hand.

The trick, I believe, is to move through the Elements from a proactive standpoint. In other words, approach with an awareness of your previous tendencies. Once you have activated the influence of the Elements in your life, you will find some of your behavior patterns and reactions to situations beginning to change. For example, if you have always found yourself to be a jealous person (and by this I mean fiercely jealous), it might have been due to a Water Element Imbalance, or perhaps a lack of balancing Earth Element. Once you balance your Water and establish and stabilize your Earth, you might find yourself more centered and peaceful, and therefore much less likely to react so strongly.

However, until this happens, we find our behavior patterns sometimes mystify us because they seem to have no rhyme or reason. Only when we stop and think through our actions do we realize what our behavior patterns have been. Following the Life Elements system, we might learn that some of these seeming inconsistencies are not in fact inconsistencies. We might find they are instead the assertion of one or another Element's influence on how we act/react to a given situation. Once we know what the Elemental influences might be, we will be better able to predict and also modify our own reactions/responses.

Let us take a look at the possible combinations of dual Element Designations. First, there is the Air/Fire Combination. This is a potentially incendiary Combination, since Air can feed Fire, particularly if the Air influence leads toward an Imbalance or if there is little Earth influence in the mix.

Air/Fire Combination

Please note: If you have received a result of a combination of Elemental influences, you are already on the path to completing the Integration Process. You are a combination of multiple Elements, so characteristics of each of them play significant roles in your life. Please read the Descriptions for each individual Element of your particular Combination. The Description of multiple Elemental influences below specifically deals with how these Elements combine and blend in your personality, rather than dealing with each Element individually.

If Air is dominant, then the actions and passions that are so much a part of the Fire Element can be mitigated by the planning and reasoning that are the domain of Air. An Air personality plans very well and reasons with logic, and then once the plan has been solidified, the action that is characteristic of Fire gets ignited and the plan is put into motion. Because Air mitigates Fire in this case, the plan is put into action very well and with constant forward momentum. If Fire is dominant, the same thing can hold true when making plans and putting them into motion; however, sometimes, especially when the situation is one about which the Fire part of the personality feels very passionate, the need to act overrides the need to plan and think through all of the possibilities. Then, sometimes, the Air part finds itself almost stuck as a spectator while the Fire part jumps in with both feet.

Generally speaking, Air will keep exerting a powerful influence of reason over the instinctive response Fire wants to give. However, there will be times when Fire runs roughshod over Air, when passions are running high. That is when the Air part of us is placed into the awkward position of watching what is happening, knowing it likely should not happen but not having quite enough influence to assert control. In other words, have you ever had the following experience? You want to buy something very badly and although you cannot really afford it, you do it anyway, even while in the back of your head a little voice is saying, *I can't really afford this. I don't need it now. I can likely find it cheaper later. I should put it aside and if I still want it next week, I'll get it then.* You almost convince yourself, but then you end up buying the item anyway. That is a perfect example of Air's reasoning trying to assert itself but Fire's active characteristics overruling Air.

Air/Fire Combination people excel at setting goals and then achieving them. If Fire is stronger, sometimes they must use the Air part of themselves to rein Fire in. In these cases, Air's influence tends to make them come to well-thought-out resolutions on which they then act appropriately. Air/Fire people have passionate natures, and yet have the cognitive inclinations to think through most of the impetuous passions to ultimately healthy resolutions. However, if Fire is too influential, then Air is sometimes used to think out the justifications for continued patterns of behavior that are not necessarily in their best interest.

This Combination also tends to brood, but Air/Fire people brood about their own impetuous choices. They over think the leaps they have taken, but the challenge is that without Water's emotional center and Earth's calming influence, they keep repeating some of these patterns despite the reasoning of their excellent minds. Unfortunately, even while they are aware that they should not have behaved in a certain manner, their Fire characteristics keep things in motion and often keep patterns going. In fact, precisely because their minds are so excellent, they might have trouble changing their ingrained patterns of behavior. They justify what they have done, and can have a very difficult time seeing a different point of view because their passionate natures make it more challenging for them to see when they have made a mistake. In other words, often, their analysis leads them to the belief they are completely in the right. This Combination has a huge stubborn streak and acts on it.

If Fire is dominant, you might find yourself having jumped in to resolve a situation even when your more analytical nature was still uncertain it was indeed the correct course of action. This will often be a source of frustration to you. These stresses will be mitigated by the more calming effects of the Earth Element, and by the increased sense of acceptance of your own status and potential flaws that come from connection to the emotional center of the Water Element.

How Do You Proceed?

Your EDAT scores dictate the order in which you will proceed.

EDAT score: Air was dominant to Fire

1. Fully develop your affiliation to Fire. Complete Fire's Missions and Meditations.
2. Cultivate Earth. Complete Earth's Missions and Meditations.
3. Cultivate Water. Complete Water's Missions and Meditations.
4. Once you have completed all of the Missions and Meditations, please go to Chapters 19 and 20 and conclude the Integration Process.

EDAT score: Fire was dominant to Air

1. Fully develop your affiliation to Air. Complete Air's Missions and Meditations.
2. Cultivate Water. Complete Water's Missions and Meditations.
3. Cultivate Earth. Complete Earth's Missions and Meditations.
4. Once you have completed all of the Missions and Meditations, please go to Chapters 19 and 20 and conclude the Integration Process.

Air/Water Combination

Please note: If you have received a result of a combination of Elemental influences, you are already on the path to completing the Integration Process. You are a combination of multiple Elements, so characteristics of each of them play significant roles in your life. Please read the Descriptions for each individual Element of your particular Combination. The Description of multiple Elemental influences below specifically deals with how these Elements combine and blend in your personality, rather than dealing with each Element individually.

The Air/Water person thinks very well, reasons out the solutions to problems and still remains open to the intuitive leaps so much a part of the Water Element. I believe Albert Einstein was an Air/Water personality. He had both the excellent mind and the facile intuition that allowed him to envision such incredible and innovative concepts. In some ways, Air/Water people have the very best of all worlds. They have access to the mind and the heart simultaneously. The analysis of Air and the emotion of Water provide an atmosphere ripe with possibilities. This Combination especially leaves itself open to new ideas, and can see the value of fresh and exciting new realms. Air/Water people can often envision the technical, but from a holistic perspective, so they might make terrific doctors or psychologists, and can be very creative as well. This creativity will be more forthcoming if Water is the more dominant of the two Elements, since Air can sometimes get mired in over thinking the creative process instead of allowing it to grow holistically. These people make excellent psychologists because they can do both the intellectual processing and the emotional support necessary for good counselors.

Air/Water people tend to over think situations and brood on what has been the subject of those thoughts. In fact, if left unchecked or unresolved, situations can become sources of obsessive thoughts and emotions. When they love, Air/Water people love deeply, sometimes to the point they can think of nothing else because the feelings overwhelm everything else going on in their lives. They might end up living with constant thoughts about the object of their desires, whether it is a person or a thing.

The Air/Water personality is the real daydreamer of the Elemental Combinations. This person has an excellent mind, one that works out issues and solutions intuitively and with reasoning. However, emotional characteristics of Water can confuse thoughts to the extent they seem to whirl out of control. In fact, emotions will fuel the stream of thoughts, and the overflow can cause a great deal of angst and confusion without the calming influence of Earth.

If this person is feeling happy, she or he might have trouble calming down, because she or he keeps generating thoughts, plans, and ideas. Each new idea flows over the one before it, and the fresh excitement of this generation of thoughts and intuitive leaps can bring energy, joy, and a sense of forward momentum. This last can be wonderful: except when it is necessary to focus or act, because the idea of forward momentum is not, in itself, actual action without the influence of Fire.

If, on the other hand, the person is already feeling sad or disappointed, this can set up a downward spiral into depression, because the mind is sharp enough to explain the feelings as being necessary, vital, and correct, whether or not they are in the best interest of the person feeling those emotions. The best way to mitigate these downward spirals is to keep coming back to positive thought patterns and using the analytical nature of the Air part of the personality. This will allow the person to think through the emotions to make peace with them, not just to let them career out of control. In this case, we do not want to add fuel to the over thinking fire. In other words, we can sometimes get so wound up in thinking about the feelings, we have trouble coming back to earth: to a stable and centered place.

From a more positive place, our emotions can be mitigated if we think through the issues. We will have a greater chance of doing so if we have sufficient mental/emotional space available.

How Do You Proceed?

Your EDAT scores dictate the order in which you will proceed.

EDAT score: Air was dominant to Water
1. Fully develop your affiliation to Water. Complete Water's Missions and Meditations.
2. Cultivate Earth. Complete Earth's Missions and Meditations.
3. Cultivate Fire. Complete Fire's Missions and Meditations.
4. Once you have completed all of the Missions and Meditations, please go to Chapters 19 and 20 and conclude the Integration Process.

EDAT score: Water was dominant to Air

1. Fully develop your affiliation to Air. Complete Air's Missions and Meditations.
2. Cultivate Fire. Complete Fire's Missions and Meditations.
3. Cultivate Earth. Complete Earth's Missions and Meditations.
4. Once you have completed all of the Missions and Meditations, please go to Chapters 19 and 20 and conclude the Integration Process.

Air/Earth Combination

Please note: If you have received a result of a combination of Elemental influences, you are already on the path to completing the Integration Process. You are a combination of multiple Elements, so characteristics of each of them play significant roles in your life. Please read the Descriptions for each individual Element of your particular Combination. The Description of multiple Elemental influences below specifically deals with how these Elements combine and blend in your personality, rather than dealing with each Element individually.

If you already have Air and Earth integrated, then you are able to think things through from a calm place. When confronted with new situations, you do not just jump in; you look inside for answers first. If answers are forthcoming, then you evaluate and analyze the situation from a more peaceful place than some of your Elemental counterparts. You still bring reason to everything, and your emotions tend not to cloud your judgment.

On the flip side, you might sometimes get lost in thinking of the practical, physical, tangible needs and factors, rather than being able to or even interested in looking at the emotional, metaphysical, or spiritual ones. Lists that are focused mostly on the practical are sources of comfort to you, and you are likely one of the most organized people you know. Order is of utmost importance, and you are a big planner. You try to make sure order stays the way you have designed in your mind.

If Air is the dominant portion of your double Designation, you believe in organizing your thoughts, and the Earth Element is there to help you turn those thoughts into reality by having the practical part of your nature be there in support of the logical part. However, it is possible for you to think, meditate, or even brood on what needs to be done, but do so in a sedentary state because of the Earth influence. If Earth is dominant, you might find yourself making plans but then not moving on them. Further, you might formulate excuses to yourself for why you have done nothing. With the Air Element being so prevalent, you are likely very good at rationalizing why something should or should not be done. The Earth influence here will most often place you squarely in a place of not doing or accomplishing much, and in addition, you will justify it to yourself believably.

If you have no Imbalances to address, your next step will be to strengthen your connection to Fire. The Fire Element will help you act on that which you have planned. The Water Element will help you establish a sense of wellbeing and a healthy emotional state, regardless of where you find yourself.

How Do You Proceed?

Your EDAT scores dictate the order in which you will proceed.

EDAT score: Air was dominant to Earth

1. Fully develop your affiliation to Earth. Complete Earth's Missions and Meditations.
2. Cultivate Fire. Complete Fire's Missions and Meditations.
3. Cultivate Water. Complete Water's Missions and Meditations.
4. Once you have completed all of the Missions and Meditations, please go to Chapters 19 and 20 and conclude the Integration Process.

EDAT score: Earth was dominant to Air

1. Fully develop your affiliation to Air. Complete Air's Missions and Meditations.

2. Cultivate Water. Complete Water's Missions and Meditations.
3. Cultivate Fire. Complete Fire's Missions and Meditations.
4. Once you have completed all of the Missions and Meditations, please go to Chapters 19 and 20 and conclude the Integration Process.

Fire/Water Combination

Please note: If you have received a result of a combination of Elemental influences, you are already on the path to completing the Integration Process. You are a combination of multiple Elements, so characteristics of each of them play significant roles in your life. Please read the Descriptions for each individual Element of your particular Combination. The Description of multiple Elemental influences below specifically deals with how these Elements combine and blend in your personality, rather than dealing with each Element individually.

This is potentially the most volatile of all of the Elemental Combinations. The passion and forward motion of Fire meet the emotional focus and source of Water. This is a time to be extremely careful and make every effort to think through important decisions, because you tend to follow your heart and act impulsively.

If Water is dominant, you have much emotional fortitude. You are able to intuit answers and then act on them. You can rely on being aware of your feelings and being able to express them. In this case, Fire's aspects of action will help you express your feelings when they need to be. However, if Fire is dominant, you might find yourself acting on your feelings rashly, and sometimes it will not be in your best interest to have done so. Your emotions stem from a deep well, and you will tend to react to stimuli with an immediate emotional response. If you were solely a Water personality, you would have your feelings about a situation but likely not act on them right away, until you had taken time to recognize exactly what they were. And if you had strong Air, you would be able to analyze your feelings before you reacted. However, without the mitigating influence of Air's reason, currently, once you have an emotional response to something, your Fire nature can take over and have you say and do things that might not be in your best interest. This happens because your emotions, passions, and actions run unchecked by the reason of Air and the centeredness of Earth.

If it is possible, when your Fire nature tries to get you to act, keep trying to access your calming emotions rather than the immediate response you are inclined to make in a given situation. As you cultivate Air and Earth, these rash tendencies will become mitigated by thought and peace, and you will have greater control over when you act.

How Do You Proceed?

Your EDAT scores dictate the order in which you will proceed.

EDAT score: Water was dominant to Fire

1. Fully develop your affiliation to Fire. Complete Fire's Missions and Meditations.
2. Cultivate Earth. Complete Earth's Missions and Meditations.
3. Cultivate Air. Complete Air's Missions and Meditations.
4. Once you have completed all of the Missions and Meditations, please go to Chapters 19 and 20 and conclude the Integration Process.

EDAT score: Fire was dominant to Water

1. Fully develop your affiliation to Water. Complete Water's Missions and Meditations.
2. Cultivate Air. Complete Air's Missions and Meditations.
3. Cultivate Earth. Complete Earth's Missions and Meditations.
4. Once you have completed all of the Missions and Meditations, please go to Chapters 19 and 20 and conclude the Integration Process.

Fire/Earth Combination

Please note: If you have received a result of a combination of Elemental influences, you are already on the path to completing the Integration Process. You are a combination of multiple Elements, so characteristics of each of them play significant roles in your life. Please read the Descriptions for each individual Element of your particular Combination. The Description of multiple Elemental influences below specifically deals with how these Elements combine and blend in your personality, rather than dealing with each Element individually.

As a Fire/Earth Combination, you are a study in contrasts. This Combination happens infrequently. Generally speaking, you are either an active sort or you are a stable, centered sort from the influence of the two Elements that designate you. Or, you have periods of extreme activity until you finally collapse from exhaustion, then have periods of extreme stillness until something sparks you to move again, and the cycle continues.

When Earth and Fire are in balance, you are centered and stable and act when the time is right. You do so from a calm certainty that this is what you are supposed to be doing in the moment. You might not always think through the plan, or have articulated for yourself exactly how you feel about the given situation. But when you do act, you do it from a centered position. The Earth aspect balances the Fire's desire to act and act now.

A Combination of the two Elements means you know when to act and you know when to rest. If you had Air influence as well, you would also have the tools of reason and logic to help you reach decisions before you act on them. (This is not to say you do not have them. It is more to say they are not immediately available because Fire's impetuous nature is so prevalent.)

On the other hand, if you dip into an Imbalance, it might be extremely frustrating for you, because you feel the urge to act but do not do so. You simply sit there being frustrated by the desire to act. The energy gets spent in other directions rather than on the very thing you want and need to accomplish. So, for example, you will spend a lot of time on the computer becoming extremely good at a game or at blogging, but not be proactive in accomplishing the well-balanced and necessary tasks the Earth part of you sets for yourself.

This works for all aspects of life. Fire/Earth people can incorporate the stillness/action of their immediate personality reflections into every part of their lives. For example, this ability to act or to be still depending on the situation will stand them in good stead in all parts of their lives: before every major change. The times it might cause difficulties are when they find themselves pulled into these two opposite directions simultaneously. Should they act or should they be still? This is when the other Elements' characteristics will be vital. Air's reasoning will help make those decisions, and Water's kindness will help make them be compassionate ones.

How Do You Proceed?

Your EDAT scores dictate the order in which you will proceed.

EDAT score: Earth was dominant to Fire
1. Fully develop your affiliation to Fire. Complete Fire's Missions and Meditations.
2. Cultivate Air. Complete Air's Missions and Meditations.
3. Cultivate Water. Complete Water's Missions and Meditations.
4. Once you have completed all the Missions and Meditations, please go to Chapters 19 and 20 and conclude the Integration Process.

EDAT score: Fire was dominant to Earth
1. Fully develop your affiliation to Earth. Complete Earth's Missions and Meditations.
2. Cultivate Air. Complete Air's Missions and Meditations.
3. Cultivate Water. Complete Water's Missions and Meditations.
4. Once you have completed all of the Missions and Meditations, please go to Chapters 19 and 20 and conclude the Integration Process.

Water/Earth Combination

Please note: If you have received a result of a combination of Elemental influences, you are already on the path to completing the Integration Process. You are a combination of multiple Elements, so characteristics of each of them play significant roles in your life. Please read the Descriptions for each individual Element of your particular Combination. The Description of multiple Elemental influences below specifically deals with how these Elements combine and blend in your personality, rather than dealing with each Element individually.

In some ways, the Water/Earth blend is one of the most stable Combinations with which to begin this Element Integration Process. As a Water/Earth person, you have solid access to your emotions. You feel them, deal with them, and are most drawn to returning to a stable, centered base once the stimulus for the emotional response has passed. While your emotions might determine your overall state of mind/feelings in any given situation, the calm center to which the Earth influence always wants to return you plays a large role in maintaining a sense of balance. Certainly, like so many of us, you wish for love and relationships in your life. However, the desire for a stable, loving, long-term relationship, one that will satisfy both the Water desire for love and connection and the Earth inclination toward peace, tranquility, and a solid foundation, will be one of the primary guiding influences in your life. Unlike with Fire, there is not so much a need for passion and adventure, and once satisfied that love is real and true, you will be most concerned with the "nesting" instinct that will produce a beautiful yet cozy and welcoming home and atmosphere.

If you do not attempt to integrate the passion and motivation of Fire, however, you might never actually seek and find the love and connection you desire. In some ways, it appears you almost wish to bypass those first few months of a relationship that are fueled by passion and infatuation. Instead, you might wish to be "settled already." If this sounds familiar to you, then next you will want to look at and study the Fire Missions and Meditations, for it is relatively common wisdom that the best way to find that stable, secure, loving, and connected relationship is to begin with those first breathless weeks and months of a new romance. Fire's passion and motivation will help you bring this into your life, so the other aspects of you, the ones that desire lifelong connection, will be satisfied.

How Do You Proceed?

Your EDAT scores dictate the order in which you will proceed.

EDAT score: Water was dominant to Earth
1. Fully develop your affiliation to Earth. Complete Earth's Missions and Meditations.
2. Cultivate Fire. Complete Fire's Missions and Meditations.
3. Cultivate Air. Complete Air's Missions and Meditations.
4. Once you have completed all of the Missions and Meditations, please go to Chapters 19 and 20 and conclude the Integration Process.

EDAT score: Earth was dominant to Water
1. Fully develop your affiliation to Water. Complete Water's Missions and Meditations.
2. Cultivate Air. Complete Air's Missions and Meditations.
3. Cultivate Fire. Complete Fire's Missions and Meditations.
4. Once you have completed all of the Missions and Meditations, please go to Chapters 19 and 20 and conclude the Integration Process.

Chapter 9
Element Imbalance Introduction and Assessment Tool

Now that you know your Element Designation, you are ready for the next step. After you have taken the EDAT in Chapter 6, and have read your Element Designation(s), complete the next section before you do anything else. Just as we have a predisposition to emanate a certain Element's characteristics in our daily lives, sometimes the influence or characteristics of one or more of the Elements plays too great a role in our lives. This can create an Element Imbalance. Thus, in addition to determining the Element Designation, it is necessary to assess any potential Element Imbalances before completing the Integration Process. The questions that follow are sometimes challenging to answer, but I encourage you to persevere and attempt to answer them as honestly as you can. Remember, no one will see the answers to these questions, so you can be as truthful as possible as you approach this portion of the assessment. Once you have completed the EIAT, you will have a much greater idea of where your Elemental challenges lie. When you know the Elemental Imbalances, you will address them with the appropriate Missions and Meditations. Once your Imbalances are addressed, from that point, you will complete the Integration Process and increase your sense of self, your sense of balance, and your sense of peace.

Please complete the EIAT in the same manner you completed the EDAT. For each statement that is generally true for you, please check the white check box in the corresponding column to the right of the statement. Once you have completed this section, you will add your score vertically down the columns by counting the number of boxes you checked in each column. In other words, you will add the number of boxes you checked that appear in Column E, and tabulate the score at the bottom of the Table. Next, you will add the boxes you checked in Column F, and then Column G, and so forth. At the end, please add the total number of check marks and enter the number in the text field in the bottom row of that column.

Please note: Many people have Element Imbalances. Part of the reason I wrote this book is to help identify and then rectify those very Imbalances. This knowledge is just a stepping-stone. From here, the adventure of changing your life begins.

If you have Internet access, you might wish to take the EIAT online. The online versions of the test is exactly the same, except the scoring is done for you. You will then be able to take the information given online and apply it here. You can access the EIAT page here: http://www.LifeElements.info. Click the "Assessments" button. Then click the "Element Imbalance Assessment Tool (EIAT)" link.

Please remember to complete this assessment with as much honesty as possible. The EDAT and EIAT are designed to give you a place to start, and I encourage you to accept your present status and not judge yourself, regardless of where your results take you. We are living, evolving, dynamic beings, and we change constantly. You will change even as you complete this assessment. In fact, the very fact that you are taking the assessment indicates you are making changes in your life. Also, you are the only one who will ever see the results, and they are specifically designed to help you with the Integration Process. To get where we are going, we all need a place to begin. This assessment is no different. You need to have a starting place. You need to know where you are now to be able to start the journey to eventually finish it as a whole and well-rounded being on this planet.

Element Imbalance Assessment Tool (EIAT)

Element Imbalance Questions	E	F	G	H
1. I tend to find myself sad at random moments and often for no apparent reason.				☐
2. I tend to be interested in accumulating material possessions.	☐			
3. I tend to jump to the worst conclusions about what people think of me.		☐		
4. I am perhaps overly concerned with having a neat home.	☐			
5. My moods can swing from one extreme to the other and sometimes quickly.				☐
6. People see me as a very stable person, but to me that just means they do not know me very well.	☐			
7. I find it difficult to find items in my home because things are not organized.			☐	
8. I find I am more sedentary than I am comfortable with.	☐			
9. Getting lost when I am driving really frustrates me.		☐		
10. Sometimes I hate to leave the house, and I have to drag myself out and about.	☐			
11. I tend to fear the truth about what people really think of me.				☐
12. I believe I have little control over the day-to-day events of my life, and my life ends up feeling chaotic.			☐	
13. I often find it hard to forgive people who have hurt my feelings, even after they apologize.				☐
14. I tend to procrastinate, especially about things that are really important to me.	☐			
15. If anything gets in the way of something I have planned, I will likely get angry.		☐		

Element Imbalance Questions	E	F	G	H
16. I tend to take on too many tasks, and then feel overwhelmed at the prospect of completing them.			☐	
17. It is extremely important to me that I am perceived as attractive.			☐	
18. Sometimes, even a random word will make me feel as if I am not likable.				☐
19. On the whole, I do not appreciate myself.	☐			
20. It is very important for me to be right.		☐		
21. I tend not to live up to responsibilities I have taken on, because I am too busy doing other things.			☐	
22. I can take it personally and get upset if people do not agree with me.		☐		
23. I tend to jump from one interest or hobby to the next.			☐	
24. I feel as if I am cut off from truly experiencing my emotions.				☐
25. I tend to start many projects, and have trouble completing a lot of them.			☐	
26. I watch more than 14 hours of television a week.	☐			
27. I can have great difficulty expressing my feelings.				☐
28. I feel ashamed of my past.	☐			
29. It is really important for me to give my opinion on any situation, even if it has not been solicited.		☐		
30. In a discussion, I will sometimes take an opposing view just because it might get people to pay attention to me.		☐		
31. I often feel like people do not get to know the real me.	☐			

Element Imbalance Questions	E	F	G	H
32. I do not feel appreciated by other people, and consequently I do not appreciate myself.				☐
33. I can be sensitive to perceived slights				☐
34. I sometimes feel like very few people even want to know who I really am.	☐			
35. Loud noises or seemingly chaotic situations can really fray my nerves.	☐			
36. When I encounter a problem in my relationship, my first instinct is to blame my partner.				☐
37. I tend to be an anxious person.			☐	
38. I often find myself in debt and living beyond my means.			☐	
39. I relish attention paid to what I say.			☐	
40. I find that my home is often a mess.			☐	
41. I tend toward depression.				☐
42. I sympathize with other people's problems to such a degree, that I feel compelled to help them even when it might be to my own detriment.				☐
43. I tend to worry a lot, especially about things over which I have no control.				☐
44. It is challenging for me to get started on projects, because I am usually too scattered or busy to finish them.			☐	
45. I tend to make rash decisions and act on them too quickly			☐	
46. I like to have many things around me, especially books and knickknacks. Some might even call me a packrat.	☐			
47. I get very upset if things are out of place in my home or at work.	☐			
48. I really enjoy it when people believe me to be an expert at something.		☐		

Element Imbalance Questions	E	F	G	H
49. In my heart of hearts, I often think people do not like me.		☐		
50. I tend to be tense and often under stress.			☐	
51. New people in my environment tend to make me withdraw.	☐			
52. Despite the fact that I am aware of my deadlines, I have a hard time motivating myself to meet them.	☐			
53. In my heart of hearts, I often feel lonely.				☐
54. Often, when I am hurt, I do not express my hurt feelings. Instead, I express anger.				☐
55. Generally, at parties, I tend to be a wallflower.	☐			
56. I have a negative self-image with respect to my physical body.	☐			
57. I spend a lot of time on random activities I believe waste time, but I cannot seem to stop.			☐	
58. I tend to jump from one relationship to the next.			☐	
59. My relationships with many of my friends tend to be based on a shared sense of drama.				☐
60. Making a good living is much more important than loving what you do.			☐	
61. I cannot seem to keep any one job for too long.			☐	
62. When in a highly emotional situation, I find it difficult to pinpoint what I really feel.				☐
63. I get frustrated very easily if friends or family do not do things the way I would like.		☐		
64. I find it difficult to let people see my true feelings.				☐
65. When I shop, I can feel compelled to buy the most expensive item whether or not it will yield the best quality for the price.	☐			

Element Imbalance Questions	E	F	G	H
66. I often act with "fake" or forced cheerfulness to hide my true state of mind.				☐
67. I tend to second-guess myself.		☐		
68. I find myself easily swayed by other people's arguments, even when I truly believe in my own opinion.		☐		
69. I can get extremely uncomfortable when there is a lot going on around me.	☐			
70. It is of utmost importance for me to be successful in anything I try.			☐	
71. I find myself insecure about my level of intelligence.		☐		
72. I tend to bear grudges.				☐
73. If someone hurts me, even unintentionally, I can be hard-pressed to let it go.				☐
74. I have trouble setting reasonable boundaries with friends who want support and help from me. I feel as if they will not like me if I do not help them.	☐			
75. I can be very apprehensive about meeting and getting to know new people.	☐			
76. I feel as if I sometimes hide my insecurity behind a brash intelligence and wit.		☐		
77. Once I make up my mind, very little will ever sway my opinion.		☐		
78. I might take revenge on those who hurt me.			☐	
79. I need deadlines or I cannot accomplish things.			☐	
80. My sad moods can last, but my happy moods can deteriorate in an instant.				☐
81. I can be a fiercely jealous person.				☐
82. It is very important to me to be more successful than my friends and colleagues.			☐	

Element Imbalance Questions	E	F	G	H
83. In my heart of hearts, I often feel aimless and like I have no real life goals or plans.	☐			
84. I might appear to be laid-back about the tasks I need to complete, but actually, I am often quite overwhelmed by all I need to accomplish.	☐			
85. Generally, I need to be the life of the party.			☐	
86. I am sometimes insecure that my friends like each other more than they like me.				☐
87. I spend a lot of time brooding over issues I have with friends, coworkers, or family, rather than addressing them with the appropriate parties.		☐		
88. With no evidence, I have thought people were talking about me behind my back.		☐		
89. I tend to enjoy gossiping.		☐		
90. I relish solving problems, and can become obsessed with them until they are resolved.		☐		
91. Although I will often find myself exhausted the following day, I feel compelled to go out with friends if I am asked to do so.			☐	
92. I have many regrets about things I have or have not done.	☐			
93. It can take me "forever" to make up my mind.		☐		
94. I find myself insecure about my own intellectual ability,		☐		
95. I feel unappreciated by the people in my life.				☐
96. I sometimes feel the need to boast about my accomplishments to others.		☐		
97. I am always looking for the next great club/ restaurant/play/show/movie, because that way, people will join me and I will not feel alone.			☐	

Element Imbalance Questions	E	F	G	H
98. It is extremely important for me to be successful, and I am willing to do just about anything to succeed.			☐	
99. I sometimes cheat to look smarter than I am.		☐		
100. I often find myself running from one drama to the next.			☐	

Totals for Column E: _____   F: _____   G: _____   H: _____

Are any of the results 12 or higher? If you did not receive a score of 12 or higher in any of the columns above, then you have no Elemental Imbalances. Please go to the Element Designation chapter for your Element (from the EDAT) to proceed with Element Integration Process. If you received a result of 12 or higher for any of the columns, then you likely have an Element Imbalance in the Element corresponding to that column. Please read the Element Imbalance descriptions for that column and review whether or not the Descriptions appear to be true for you. If you have two sections that yield scores higher than 12, then you have a combination of Imbalances. Please read your individual Element Imbalance Description for each Element Imbalance you score (Chapter 10). Then, please read the appropriate Combination section as well (Chapter 11).

The Element Imbalance for Column E is **Earth**. Please turn to page 93 to read the Earth Imbalance characteristics. These characteristics should describe some of your tendencies and challenges.

The Element Imbalance for Column F is **Air**. Please turn to page 96 to read the Air Imbalance characteristics. These characteristics should describe some of your tendencies and challenges.

The Element Imbalance for Column G is **Fire**. Please turn to page 99 to read the Fire Imbalance characteristics. These characteristics should describe some of your tendencies and challenges.

The Element Imbalance for Column H is **Water**. Please turn to page 102 to read the Water Imbalance characteristics. These characteristics should describe some of your tendencies and challenges.

My note to you: As I was writing this book, I was asked if there was any value to simply knowing and then cultivating your strongest Element. In other words, once you have taken the EDAT and EIAT, you might find out Fire is your strongest and most easily accessible Element. I believe there is value to be found in knowing what your strongest and most instinctive reactions will be to any given situation in your life. If you are a Fire person, then your instinctual reactions to situations most likely will be ones of action: passionate action. You will immediately act upon the stimuli presented to you. However, there might be times when acting or reacting immediately is not the most appropriate response. There might be times when having the ability to step back and assess the present situation with a clear and reasoning mind might be preferable to simply reacting in whatever manner your passions currently take you. That is one of the times when you want to have access to the Air Element's processes of thought and reason.

If you are not naturally inclined to do so because of your fiery nature, then you will need to forge your inclination toward access to those thought processes to strengthen your connection with Air. Then, when a situation presents itself where an Air response of thought and reason is the most appropriate, you will have access to those processes despite the fact it is not your current instinctive response. Thus, even if your instinct is to react with action because of your affinity with Fire, a cultivated Air Element will enable you to step back, breathe, and assess the situation with a more rational mind. Then, because you have assessed the situation, you will find you can put your strength in Fire to use by acting when the time is right and doing so with a well-thought-out set of actions.

Thus, once you are done with the EDAT and EIAT assessments, you might certainly stop there if you wish because, at the very least, you will have ascertained where you sit in relation to the Elements. In other words, you will have gained some insight as to why you find yourself thinking, feeling, acting, and reacting as you do. If, for example, you have an Earth Imbalance, you might consistently have trouble acting on your intents. There is no blame to be laid here, but reasons that exist to explain why you have that challenge. If you have a Fire Imbalance, you might find yourself flitting from one relationship to the next or from one interest to the next without stopping and spending quality time on any of them. A Water Imbalance might keep you constantly emotionally off-kilter, and while you might feel incredibly strong emotions, they might come out in the form of wide mood swings, or you might be unable to express your feelings as you have them. An Air Imbalance might keep you over thinking the smallest details of conversations or events and while you might be able to think things through, you might be unable to make decisions or come to terms about appropriate responses.

The reason we want to address any Imbalances is so we can begin to cultivate all of the Elements evenly, with none holding particular sway over the others. While I believe there is great value to be derived in knowing your current Elemental strengths, the greatest benefits come when you use this knowledge as your starting point to Elemental Integration.

Chapter 10
Element Imbalance Descriptions

Column E: Earth Imbalance Description
Please note: These Designations are general descriptions of personality types.

If you have an Earth Imbalance, this means your natural stable, centered manner of being has dipped into too great a dependence on Earth characteristics. For example, rather than simply being able to remain peaceful and centered and not requiring constant stimulation to keep yourself engaged, you might drop into being sedentary, set in your ways, and perhaps unwilling to act when the time is appropriate to do so. In other words, the very stability you might exhibit and feel as an Earth Designation can become a liability. Instead of being centered and at peace, you might become inactive and allow your life to become monotonous. You might shy away from challenges, and be unwilling or unable to do the very things you wish to do to pursue your own happiness.

An Earth Imbalance takes Earth Element characteristics and turns them up, as it were. Whereas an Earth person might be practical, an Earth Imbalance person might be too conservative and too unwilling to take risks. This person will miss opportunities because she or he is waiting for the next big thing (and unfortunately, she or he will likely not reach for it then either). An Earth Designation person might be able to stand firm and solid in the knowledge she or he is right, but an Earth Imbalance person can be obstinate and very stubborn, and can turn away from compromise. She or he might find himself or herself quite sedentary and unwilling to move.

Earth Imbalance people will find themselves settling for the routine, and for small gains. They will focus on what is going wrong—the worst case. In other words, instead of being realistic, Earth Imbalance people dip into being pessimistic.

Rather than simply being careful and diligent, Earth Imbalance people can be too focused and almost grim in their approach to problem solving.

Mitigating an Earth Imbalance

First, you will want to acknowledge your positive Earth characteristics. Generally, people who have an Imbalance in an Element will also find they are strong in the positive characteristics of that Element as well. Thus, we must come to terms with where we are right now. So, one of the first things we need to do is to go back and reacquaint ourselves with the more positive aspects of the Earth Element. Earth Element people are centered and stable rather than sedentary. Earth Element people are realistic, and their peaceful natures keep that realism from becoming pessimism or other negative attributes. (Please return to the section describing Earth's characteristics to see how a balanced Earth Element person is described.)

To refocus onto the more positive aspects of where you are right now, go to page 150 and complete the "Guided Meditation to the Earth Element." Once you have completed the Meditation for Earth, we will look at Earth's polar opposite, Fire. Finding Fire's passion, motivation, and sense of fun and play can be incredibly helpful in mitigating an Earth Imbalance. Fire governs action, passion, creativity, sex, sexuality, and forward motion. These are the very things you will want to bring into your life to help you see things differently, act when the time is right, and move forward creatively and passionately.

Right now you are likely most inclined to sit, and to be still to the point that you might be spending an inordinate amount of time either alone, watching television, or simply sitting around. You might have even been feeling like you have been sleepwalking through your life, because few things get you excited or delighted. If you have been feeling like a spectator in your own life because everything feels routine, then Fire's spark is what you need. Together, we will ignite your anticipation of what is to come.

It is time to wake up and begin to live, really live your life. This is why you will cultivate Fire first. Since you have likely found yourself sedentary, I congratulate you on getting to this place of doing something about your situation. I recognize how difficult it must have been to begin. I know it can feel impossible to make lasting changes. It might even feel like you are swimming through molasses to get anything accomplished. However, I believe it is possible to create a pattern of forward motion regardless of where you are now. I know you can do it, as long as you take it slowly and begin to move forward one step at a time. Gradually, you will begin to create an atmosphere of change. Remember to be gentle with yourself as you embark on this process. It is more challenging for you than it is for others, but take heart that you have gotten this far.

Once you have cultivated Fire energy by completing the Fire Missions, take the EIAT again to see if your Earth Imbalance Score is lower, and therefore your Earth Imbalance is being addressed. You can repeat this process a number of times as you incorporate Fire characteristics into your life. If you do, go back to the Fire Missions and complete them again. Keep working with the Element, and you will begin to notice changes. You will find your creative spark, and it will become easier to take subsequent steps. At some point, you will find you no longer have the Earth Imbalance. You will find yourself motivated to move forward, and after Fire, you will take steps to integrate Air and then Water into your life by completing the Air and Water Missions and Meditations.

Finally, complete all of the Earth Missions to acclimate to the positive characteristics of the Earth Element. Eventually, you will balance the Elements and live a fully passionate, creative life.

How do you proceed?

Order in which to complete the Missions and Meditations from here: Fire, Air, Water, Earth

- To honor your positive Earth Element characteristics, please go to page 150 to complete the "Guided Meditation to the Earth Element."

- To begin addressing your Earth Imbalance by completing the Fire Missions and Meditations, go to page 199.
- To read another Element Imbalance Description, go to page 96 for Air, 99 for Fire, and 102 for Water.
- To read an Imbalance Combination Description, please go to Chapter 11.

Column F: Air Imbalance Description

Please note: These Designations are general descriptions of personality types.

If you have an Air Imbalance, this means your natural thought-oriented manner has dipped into too great a dependence on Air characteristics. For example, rather than simply looking at all facets of a situation, you are not satisfied until every single possible scenario has been thoroughly analyzed many times. Your desire for truth might become an extreme reliance on it. As such, if someone is less than truthful, it can be devastating to you. The very analytical nature and love of thought and reason that describe an Air Designation can become over analysis of everyday things and conversations. An Air Imbalance person might find him or herself over thinking things to the point that she or he becomes unable either to take a stand or do anything about what is occurring.

Instead of being blunt and straightforward, Air Imbalance people might dip into being tactless and sometimes rude. They might not show awareness of or care for the feelings of others. Although Air Imbalance people will often be very intelligent, they might not exhibit "street-smarts" or common sense. They tend to be very opinionated, to the point of being overbearing with those opinions. They can have an overarching need to be right, and can have many challenges if others disagree.

Air Imbalance people might be quite critical and sarcastic. They might have thought through their position on things to the point of being intolerant of other viewpoints. They believe they are correct, and leave little room for dissenting opinions.

Mitigating an Air Imbalance

First, you will want to acknowledge your positive Air characteristics. Air Element people are intelligent and thoughtful, rather than overly analytical and domineering. An Air Element person is mindful, but the thoughtfulness that allows him or her to move forward from a well-reasoned place does not run into criticism and sarcasm. If the Air Designation dips into an Imbalance, some of those positive aspects transform into their shadow selves. Thus, first, you will want to study and acknowledge your positive Air characteristics. Generally, people who have an Imbalance in an Element will also find they are strong in the positive characteristics of that Element as well. We must come to terms with where we are right now. So, one of the first things we need to do is to go back and reacquaint ourselves with the more positive aspects of the Air Element. Air Element people are reason and thought-oriented rather than anxious and prone to over analysis. An Air Element person is analytical, but his or her thoughtful, mindful nature keeps that analysis from becoming anxiety or worry. (Here, please take a look at the Air characteristics on page 59 to see how a balanced Air Element person is described).

Go to page 155 and complete the "Guided Meditation to the Air Element." This will help you refocus onto more positive aspects of where you are right now. Then we will look at Air's polar opposite, Water.

This is the basic question for you to consider: Do you find yourself worried or anxious, and perhaps even afraid of all the possibilities out there? This is not unusual with Air Imbalance people. Because their minds move so quickly and understand so much, the sheer size of what they see and understand can create an atmosphere of worry and anxiety. The other part of this is that an Air Imbalance person often keeps his or her real emotions at arm's length. The Air Imbalance person might think about what she or he feels, but seldom takes the time actually to feel it. It is easier and fulfills the pattern more quickly if the Air Imbalance person does not take too much energy to feel, but rather thinks about what she or he might feel, or worries about what other people are thinking or feeling. Seldom does this person take the time to be honest about what is going on within his or her heart. It feels too vulnerable, and therefore is avoided at all cost.

This is why I encourage you to cultivate your emotions. You will want to slow down and look at what is inside your heart. Our hearts communicate with us all the time, but Air Imbalance people tend not to listen because what might be there might be too frightening. This, however, is precisely what we must attempt to do. We must open to and allow those feelings of vulnerability. They are best cultivated by opening ourselves to the emotional center of the Water Element. Open your heart to the feelings inside you, and acknowledge and claim those feelings as valid.

You will want to incorporate these feelings slowly, and in as safe an environment as you can create. You will first want to open yourself to the Water Element by completing the "Guided Meditation to the Water Element" on page 164. Spend a bit of time getting to know your emotional center. Begin to listen to your heart. Then, once you have completed the Meditation, move on to the first Water Mission, and then the next, until you have completed them all. You will find that the Water Missions and Meditations help alleviate your Air Imbalance. It will not happen overnight, but it will happen.

When you have completed the Water Missions, take the EIAT again to see if your Air Imbalance score is lower and therefore the Imbalance is being addressed. You can repeat this process a number of times as you incorporate these balancing Water characteristics into your life. Once the Imbalance is addressed, you can go to the chapter for your Air Element Designation and continue to develop and grow in the Elements in the most appropriate order for you.

How do you proceed?

Order in which to complete the Missions and Meditations from here: Water, Fire, Earth, Air

- To honor your positive Air Element characteristics, please go to page 155 to complete the "Guided Meditation to the Air Element."
- To begin addressing your Air Imbalance by completing the Water Missions and Meditations, go to page 211.

- To read another Element Imbalance Description, go to page 99 for Fire, 102 for Water, and 93 for Earth.
- To read an Imbalance Combination Description, please go to Chapter 11.

Column G: Fire Imbalance Description

Please note: These Designations are general descriptions of personality types.

If you have a Fire Imbalance, this means your natural active, passionate, and sometimes-impulsive manner has dipped into too great a dependence on Fire characteristics. For example, rather than being on the go and sometimes leaping before you look, you appear to be in constant motion with hardly any time for repose or calm. In other words, the very passionate, fiery nature that describes a Fire Designation can become the frenetic pace and obsessive nature of a Fire Imbalance.

Instead of simply having a zest for life, a Fire Imbalance person can become obsessively in need of new challenges and stimulation. Instead of simply being willing to take risks, a Fire Imbalance person can be reckless and rash. These people have trouble being still, and often find themselves jumpy if there is no new, grand adventure to be had. They can focus their lives on passionate/sexual conquests rather than on potentially more meaningful, stable relationships.

Fire Imbalance people might have a bad temper, and might not show good judgment about when to show that temper. They can be daredevils in their approach to life, and will make things happen on their own terms, whether or not those things are appropriate.

Their love for adventure can easily become a reluctance or inability to be still. It can become a compulsive need to have excitement in their lives, and they make a habit of leaping before they look.

Mitigating a Fire Imbalance

First, you will want to study and incorporate the positive aspects of Fire characteristics, and focus on getting to the root stimuli for acting from the passionate Fire perspective. Fire Element people are passionate, adventurous, creative, and dynamic. However, their passions can be mitigated by the fact that they are willing to work hard to achieve their goals. In other words, to them, life is not just about play and passion and drama. It can also be about achieving goals, and about being willing and interested in working toward the higher good. (Please go to page 60 to read the Fire Element description.)

With a state of Imbalance, your fiery, passionate, always-on-the-go nature has dipped into a chaotic existence that likely feels overly dramatic and full of unresolved tension. You might be running from drama to drama, with little peace or time to find peace. So, one of the first things we need to do is to go back and reacquaint ourselves with the more positive aspects of the Fire Element. We need to access passion without obsession, and motion without chaos. As a Fire Imbalance person, both sides of Fire exist in you. Let us refocus on the positive.

Go to page 159 and complete the "Guided Meditation to the Fire Element." This will help you refocus onto more positive aspects of where you are right now, and will begin your journey of finding equilibrium in your Element.

Once you have acknowledged where you currently sit, you will want to move forward gently. The second part is the more active part, and your basic Fire nature might want to rush in and begin. However, you want to accomplish this task from a place of peace so as not to continue the pattern of rash forward motion. So, here, it is necessary to look at Fire's polar opposite, Earth.

Finding Earth's sense of stability and grounding can be incredibly helpful in mitigating a Fire Imbalance. Earth governs the home, the hearth, stability, security, and a feeling of centeredness and pragmatism. These are the very things you will want to bring into your life to help you see things differently, to find serenity, calm, and a sense of peace. If you cultivate Earth Element characteristics, then you will enable yourself to find your path from a stable place. The dramas that might so affect your life right now will cease to have such prominence.

Right now, you are most inclined to run, to be in perpetual motion without taking time to assess what you think and how you feel. You are likely solely in reaction mode, because that is what Fire does. You might have been experiencing too much stress, and you might be afraid there is no help or hope for resolving any of the issues that currently demand your attention. It is time to slow down, find your center, and begin the process of Element Integration. I recognize that it can feel impossible to make lasting changes, because the dramas in your life always seem to spur you to action. It might even feel like you run from one fire to the next, and you never really feel like you have the time to slow down and smell the roses, as it were.

I believe it is possible to create a pattern of positive forward motion regardless of where you are now. However, first, you must find your starting point. You must locate your center, and that is best accomplished by recognizing where you are now and then finding your stability, practicality, and commitment through the Earth Element. I know you can do it as long as you take the time to slow down, find your center, and move from there. Then, you will make changes from a calm and centered place.

When you have completed the Earth Missions and Meditations, take the EIAT to see if your Fire Imbalance score is lower, and therefore your Imbalance is being addressed. You can repeat this process a number of times as you incorporate Earth characteristics into your life. Once you have incorporated positive Earth characteristics, you will want to move on to the positive characteristics of Air, and then Water, by completing the Air and Water Missions and Meditations. Last, you will want to complete the Fire Missions to absorb and acknowledge your positive Fire characteristics.

How do you proceed?

Order in which to complete the Missions and Meditations from here: Earth, Air, Water, Fire

- To honor your positive Fire Element characteristics, please go to page 159 to complete the "Guided Meditation to the Fire Element."
- To begin addressing your Fire Imbalance by completing the Earth Missions and Meditations, go to page 185.

- To read another Element Imbalance Description, go to page 96 for Air, 102 for Water, and 93 for Earth.
- To read an Imbalance Combination Description, please go to Chapter 11.

Column H: Water Imbalance Description

Please note: These Designations are general descriptions of personality types.

If you have a Water Imbalance, this means your natural intuitive, emotion-centered manner of being has dipped into too great a dependence on Water characteristics. For example, rather than being able to access your emotions, be true to them, and operate from a place of kindness and compassion, you might find yourself very easily upset. You might also be too in-tune with the issues and problems of the people around you, and it might be difficult to erect boundaries so you can find a sense of emotional equilibrium. In other words, the very intuitive, compassionate, emotional nature that describes a Water Designation can become the hypersensitive, potentially overly dramatic nature of a Water Imbalance.

Instead of having full access to and expression of their emotions, Water Imbalance people can be overemotional, temperamental, and depressed. Their flights of fancy can develop into inordinate amounts of time spent in idle daydreaming. They can ride a perpetual emotional roller coaster with wide and quick mood swings. They can take offense very easily, and a perceived slight will affect them to large degrees. They fall in love quickly, and can show a lack of sound judgment in their choices of partners. And if or when their love is not returned, they can have a difficult time handling the situation. Because of their enhanced love of beauty, Water Imbalance people will sometimes have trouble facing unpleasant situations.

Water Imbalance people also tend toward overly critical self-assessment and self-examination. They can have an overactive imagination, particularly as it pertains to their approach to their own lives and their relationships.

Mitigating a Water Imbalance

First, you will want to look at and acknowledge your positive Water characteristics. Water Element people are compassionate, emotional, intuitive, and caring. This compassion allows Water people to sense and accept both their own feelings and the feelings of others. It allows them to view situations from a more peaceful place, rather than simply reacting from the increased emotional dynamic of a Water Imbalance. In other words, to Water Designation people, life is not just about their own emotions and states of being. It can also be about awareness of and kindness to others. (Here, please go to page 62 to read the Water Element description.)

With a Water Imbalance, your emotional, caring, intuitive nature has dipped into hypersensitivity and a lack of boundaries. You might be very easily upset, both for yourself and for others. These constant, deeply emotional ordeals might make it difficult for you to reason clearly and make thoughtful decisions. You might have already been feeling like you are too extended and too many depend on you, and that you have very little emotional fortitude left for yourself.

This constant state of internal tug-of-war indicates it is time to go back and reacquaint yourself with the more positive aspects of the Water Element. You *can* access emotion without hypersensitivity, and caring without bleeding yourself dry. As a Water Imbalance person, both sides of Water exist in you. Take the time to refocus on the positive aspects of where you are right now. It is time to reclaim your calm emotions; these are the ones that will help you complete the journey to emotional equilibrium.

Go to page 164 and complete the "Guided Meditation to the Water Element." Once you have acknowledged where you currently sit by visiting with Water, you will want to move forward deliberately and thoughtfully, so your emotions do not overtake your desire to proceed. The second part is the more step-by-step part, and your basic Water nature might tug you away from the deliberate work that needs to be done. You want to accomplish this task thoughtfully and with feelings of calm deliberation, so as not to disturb your already fragile emotional state. So here, it is necessary to look at Water's polar opposite, Air.

Finding Air's analytical approach and sense of mindfulness can be incredibly helpful in mitigating a Water Imbalance. Air governs thought, intelligence, reason, truth, and honesty. These are the very things you will want to bring into your life to help you find a sense of reasoned calm and awareness. When you cultivate Air Element characteristics, you will enable yourself to find your path thoughtfully. The challenging moods that might so affect your life right now will cease to have such prominence. Right now, you are likely most inclined to be sensitive, moody, and wrenched by the slightest things. Despite the fact that it might be difficult, it would be of great benefit to you to step back as best you can, so you can give some thought to your current state. This thoughtful state will help ease some of the emotional pressure you are under. It is opening the steam valve, as it were.

You might have been experiencing too much stress and pressure, and you might be afraid there is no help or hope for resolving any of the emotion-laden issues currently demanding your attention. It is time to slow down and give mindful attention to what sits in front of you. With reason, you will begin to find your center and begin the process of Element Integration. I recognize that it can feel impossible to make lasting changes because the dramas in your life always seem to cause you grief. You might even feel like each new challenge is just too much to handle, because they so emotionally affect you. However, I believe it is possible to create a pattern of thoughtful and deliberate assessment of your status. Each new bit of stimulation yields a reaction, and yet, I believe it is possible to approach each new challenge mindfully.

Take some time right now and do the "Guided Meditation to the Air Element" on page 155. You will want to begin to cultivate a calm, thoughtful space in your life so you can begin to feel Air's influence and bring it to you. Once you are more present in Air, you will begin to notice you are able to move forward thoughtfully, and even though you are still emotionally driven, you will no longer react from raw feeling. Instead, you will find you are more able to think through the situations in which you find yourself. Through Air's mindfulness, you will begin to approach things from a calmer and more reasoned perspective.

When you have completed the Air Missions and Meditations, take the EIAT again to see if your Water Imbalance score is lower and therefore your Imbalance is being addressed. You can repeat this process a number of times as you incorporate Air characteristics into your life. You will likely note that the score is lower, and you will begin to find a sense of peace as you then incorporate Earth's sense of stability. From this place of peace, you will be able to move forward with Fire's creativity when the time is right.

How do you proceed?

Order in which to complete the Missions and Meditations from here: Air, Earth, Fire, Water

- To honor your positive Water Element characteristics, please go to page 164 to complete the "Guided Meditation to the Water Element."
- To begin addressing your Water Imbalance by completing the Air Missions and Meditations, go to page 173.
- To read another Element Imbalance Description, go to page 96 for Air, 99 for Fire, and 93 for Earth.
- To read the Imbalance Combination Description, please go to Chapter 11.

Chapter 11
Imbalance Combination Descriptions

Some people will find multiple Imbalances when they complete the EIAT. Just as someone might have more than one Element Designation, it is possible to have more than one Imbalance. The following Imbalance Descriptions characterize specific Imbalance Combinations. In many ways, an Imbalance Combination is the mirror opposite of the Designation Combination. A Designation Combination puts a person a bit farther on the path along the Integration Process. An Imbalance Combination creates extra challenges in mitigating the Elemental Imbalances and creating a well-rounded existence. Because each Element Combination creates a unique set of characteristics, we will have to alleviate the Combination Imbalances in a pattern individual to each Imbalance Combination. Thus, those people with Combination Imbalances will have a specific set of guidelines to follow to complete the Integration Process.

First, read the individual Imbalances. Then, read the Combination Imbalance, and then please follow the appropriate instructions included within each of the Combination Imbalance Descriptions. Please note, although a person with a Combination Imbalance has a more challenging journey ahead, it is by no means impossible to complete the Integration Process. In fact, I venture to say that someone who has farther to go to complete it will accomplish this process more fully.

Air/Fire Imbalance Description

Just as there is in any of the Element Combinations, there will be much overlap between individual Air and Fire Imbalances for an Air/Fire Imbalance Combination. The Descriptions of each of those individual Elements will be very helpful in detailing the state of being of the person with this Imbalance Combination. However, this Combination will have a few unique characteristics. Earlier, we discussed the Air and Fire Imbalances individually. We noted that at their most acute, Air Imbalance people tend to over think and frantically worry, especially about things over which they have no control. Fire Imbalance people tend to run from one drama to the next. A Fire/Air Imbalance person worries about impossibilities, and then runs around trying to prepare for them and attempting to do things that will help before they are ever needed. There is always so much going on in the mind of an Air Imbalance person, and the urge to run and act and do something *right now* that Fire adds into the mix is downright "crazy-making" (the concept of crazy-making is attributed here to Julia Cameron, author of *The Artist's Way*).

Air/Fire Imbalance people are usually very intelligent, and can think through and solve many issues as long as those issues remain in the realm of the intellectual. They can often multitask and get an incredible number of tasks completed, until the day when it all falls apart because of the one thing that escaped the Air characteristics' notice: Fire was too busy pulling the person into hurrying up and acting on whatever was going on. Then, because these people are missing the center and grounding of the Earth Element, they can blow up and release a pretty cutting temper. Getting an Air/Fire person angry is not quite as big as getting a Water/Fire Imbalance angry, but it is close. Air/Fire Imbalance people can know just what buttons to push to elicit a desired response. Also, if they find themselves stressed by a situation, and when they are pushed to it, they might use their facile minds to create trouble for those who have pushed them to do so.

Mitigating an Air/Fire Imbalance

The first thing to do to mitigate an Air/Fire Imbalance is to curtail the Fire Imbalance-fueled actions being taken. We must minimize the consequences of actions taken due to this Fire Imbalance. Since Fire is the action Element, its influence is what urges us to act and act right now, regardless of whether we have thought through what must be done. An Air/Fire Imbalance throws worry and anxiety into the mix. Some people with an Air/Fire Imbalance find themselves over planning every detail, and then anxiously attempting to do too much. Thus, to begin to fix the Imbalance, we must first curb the urge to do something, anything, right now. We must find some stability and calm in the midst of whatever situations we find ourselves.

A significant part of stabilizing this particular Imbalance is to slow down both the mind and the body. The Air Imbalance makes you think and worry constantly. The Fire Imbalance makes you act to try to fix things, but often you simply cause yourself extra anxiety because, regardless of whatever you try, you remain worried and unsure. Thus, you might run around like the proverbial headless chicken, or you might find yourself extremely busy and overcommitted and yet still have little satisfaction in your social life. It is hard to be satisfied when your instincts constantly pull you onward, so you likely seldom congratulate yourself on a job well done because even if you complete your tasks, you likely still spent a great deal of energy in doing so. Further, you likely have little or no sense of stability and contentment, because regardless of how the rest of your life is going, you are seldom content and are often looking for what might be around the corner.

Once you begin to slow some of the processes going on internally and externally, you will find it easier to release some of your worry because you feel more centered and calm. Thus, first, we ease the Fire Imbalance, and then we will deal with Air.

You will want to achieve at least a temporary sense of calm by completing the Earth Meditation: "Grounding" on page 185. This will give you some time and perspective to acknowledge your current circumstances. Then, you will begin to alleviate the Imbalance by working through all of the Earth Missions. Go to page 188 and read through the Missions. See which Mission feels like it is one you might be able to do. Some of you might see your competitive streak come to life here, so you might wish immediately to do the one that sounds the most challenging. Certainly, that is one of the methods you might choose. However, sometimes jumping into the most challenging one might work, and sometimes it might backfire. If you jump into the most challenging one right away, you might find you might not complete it, or you will go "whole hog" as it were. And then the very idea of calming the Fire Imbalance will be a bit muddied as your extremely competitive, overly hectic nature will keep you from fully experiencing the stabilizing benefits of the Earth Missions and Meditations.

As you read through the Missions, please take a few deep breaths and really identify which might be one you can complete and still feel good about. You will eventually want to complete all of the Earth Missions and Meditations, to achieve the center only Earth characteristics can give you. Yet, the very act of carefully choosing a Mission is part of calming the Fire Imbalance. When you establish a solid foundation in Earth Element characteristics, you will begin to notice you have a greater sense of peace and serenity. The sense of peace will not come immediately, but if you persevere, you will find that you increasingly remain calmer and more content. The urge to run from one thing to the next will begin to subside, and when this occurs, there will be room to incorporate the positive aspects of your fiery nature. Earth Missions are incredibly helpful in mitigating a Fire Imbalance precisely *because* they ask you to slow down and achieve a sense of peace.

Once you have completed the Earth Missions and given yourself an opportunity to even out the Fire Imbalance, you will want to begin to mitigate the Air Imbalance. Just as a Fire Imbalance is best addressed by its polar opposite, Earth, an Air Imbalance is best alleviated by using the positive aspects of Water. You will want to incorporate positive Water characteristics by completing the Water Missions and Meditations. When you have smoothed out some of the Air Imbalance with Water, you will then be able to integrate some of the positive aspects of mindfulness from a place of calm.

Ideally, once you have dealt with each of these Imbalances, you will have brought the positive aspects of both Earth and Water into your life. You already had strength in Air and Fire before you began this process; however, these Elements provided you with too many of their less-than-positive characteristics. You then mitigated those characteristics by focusing on the positive aspects of Air and Fire's polar opposites. Now, you are ready to create an atmosphere ripe for growth and integration.

The next step in this process will be to address any lingering Air/Fire Imbalance issues with a reevaluation of your EDAT and EIAT. Assess your Designations and any Imbalances by completing the EDAT and EIAT again. Take note if you still receive any Element Imbalances. If so, you will want to return to the Missions and Meditations. However, this time, focus on the Missions and Meditations for Air and Fire. When you complete the Air Missions, please focus on maximizing Air's thoughtful, planning, reasoning, and analytical characteristics during the process. When you complete the Fire Missions and Meditations, focus on maximizing Fire's passionate, active, vibrant characteristics during the process. This will give you access to the positive aspects of these two Elements, even as their characteristics are tempered by your newfound strength in Water and Earth.

Please note: This is not an overnight process. It will take some time to incorporate and create new patterns of behavior and thought. I encourage you to accept where you are right now without judgment, and then move forward from here. Do not be surprised if your second EDAT score yields multiple Element Designations (and also eventually decreases your Imbalance scores to zero). When you begin to integrate the Elements through the Missions and Meditations, you take on more of their characteristics, and more of them are available to you in beneficial ways. Remember, we want to imbue ourselves with all of their positive aspects, so this is a desirable outcome.

When you have completed all of the Missions and Meditations, assess your Designation one last time. Ideally, you will want to have scored so all four Elements are present in your EDAT. If there are any not present, you will want to return to those Elements' Missions and Meditations and complete them again as you focus on their most positive aspects. Increasingly, you will find you are more able to identify the Elements working in your life.

   Once you have fully developed each of the Elements, please go to Chapters 19 and 20. Read through how to incorporate the Elements into your daily life, and then complete the "Meditation to Honor Your Completion of the Integration Process." This last part of the Integration Process will help you feel more complete and whole. You will then be free and open to live your life on your own terms, secure in the knowledge that you have a stable foundation, emotional health, creative passion, and mindfulness.

How do you proceed?

- To find peace and grounding before you proceed, go to the Earth Meditation: "Grounding" on page 185.
- To honor your positive Fire Element characteristics, please go to page 159 to complete the "Guided Meditation to the Fire Element."
- To begin to address the Fire Imbalance with Earth Missions, go to page 188.
- To honor your positive Air Element characteristics, please go to page 155 to complete the "Guided Meditation to the Air Element."
- To begin to address your Air Imbalance with Water Missions and Meditations, go to page 211.
- To reassess your Elements, go to the EDAT on page 48 or the EIAT on page 83.

Air/Water Imbalance Description

   A person who has an Air/Water Imbalance can be in for some challenging times. The Air Imbalance tendency to overanalyze a situation becomes even more pronounced when it occurs in conjunction with the fierce emotional propensities of Water Imbalance characteristics. The two Imbalances and their characteristic counterparts tend to make it extremely challenging to resolve issues and move forward. For example, when a person who has an Air/Water Imbalance is emotionally hurt, she or he stews in those emotions, thinks about them in myriad ways, and has a difficult time letting go of slights. In fact, the events in this person's life can take on great significance simply because they are experienced. The urge to over think and over feel can be so strong, it creates a self-perpetuating cycle of intense feelings and subsequent over analysis of those feelings. Whereas an Air/Water-designated person might find a balance between the need to analyze and deal with feelings, an Air/Water Imbalance person might overanalyze both the situation and his or her feelings to the point that she or he will seethe about it until she or he experiences loss of control. This Imbalance does not have the stability of Earth to keep it centered, or Fire to help act and do whatever needs to be done to resolve the situation. So, an Air/Water Imbalance might simply make the person feel an incredible amount of emotion and have a lot of thoughts and worries about a given situation. However, she or he can neither act nor come to a sense of peace about what is happening.

Generally, when mitigating an Imbalance, we want to look at the polar opposite of the Element Imbalance we are attempting to mitigate. In this case, however, the two Imbalances are already polar opposites, since usually we would equalize an Air Imbalance with Water Missions and Meditations, and vice versa. Thus, any time there is an Imbalance of polar opposite Elements (Fire/Earth or Air/Water), this creates a particularly volatile set of characteristics. This means we must develop a new paradigm for dealing with the Imbalance. However, before that can occur, it is crucial that we acknowledge this Imbalance plays a role in our lives. Once we name an issue in our lives, it becomes much easier to begin to resolve it.

The Air/Water Imbalance person brings to the table an incredible ability to think through and analyze whatever situation is at hand. The Air Imbalance portion of this takes all that thinking and turns it to the negative. If there is a problem to be handled, for example, an Air Imbalance person will come to it with the belief that there are too many facets and possibilities. The Water portion of this will begin to feel daunted, and will begin to feed into the idea that there is no way this individual can handle, deal with, and successfully complete whatever needs to be done. It is an insidious path, because it feeds back upon itself.

Put simply: You think you can't do it. Water tells you can't. You begin to feel bad about yourself. You keep having negative self-talk, and sure enough, you paralyze yourself with negative thought patterns and self-doubt to the point that nothing gets done. And then you do not handle the situation, and then you feel even worse. If this sounds familiar, then you are moving in rhythm with the Imbalance the EIAT indicated. More importantly, there is something you can do to resolve it.

First, regardless of your current situation, I encourage you to initiate some activities that will bring some peace and serenity to your life. It is difficult and often almost impossible to make changes that are permanent and for the highest good when approaching these changes from a place of chaos. When we attempt to handle situations from this non-balanced perspective we have a tendency to shoot first and ask questions later, even if the only thing we are "shooting" is our own dreams, desires, or hopes. The turn toward negative thought patterns happens to all of us, and yet the Air/Water Imbalance creates an atmosphere that is fertile ground for self-defeating thoughts.

Mitigating an Air/Water Imbalance

Just like an Earth/Fire Imbalance, an Air/Water Imbalance consists of a combination of polar opposites. This is a slightly more challenging Imbalance Combination to resolve. While the other Imbalances can be resolved with the Elements that are naturally inclined to mitigate them, in this case, the mitigating Elements are the ones out of balance. This can make the person with the Imbalance feel as if little is in his or her control. Things might feel off-kilter and too unstable. It is hard to make lasting, positive changes if there is no stable base from which to build. So the first thing you need to do is to find a sense of calm and serenity.

The best way to find serenity is to incorporate some positive Earth Element energy into your life. It will be of great benefit to you to complete the Earth Meditation: "Grounding" on page 185. Also, take time to do projects with your hands. (Woodworking, knitting, and gardening are terrific Earth activities.) Whenever we work with our physical bodies, we are accessing the Earth Element. Keep your focus on the process of doing whatever you decide to do, and allow your thoughts to focus only on the task at hand.

Earth energy brings awareness, centering, and serenity to you. That becomes necessary in going through any step-by-step process to make a change you want to make and feel strong enough to make. When you establish a solid foundation in Earth Element characteristics, you will begin to notice you have a greater sense of peace and serenity. The sense of peace will not come immediately, but if you persevere, you will increasingly find that you remain calmer and more content.

A significant part of stabilizing this particular Imbalance is to slow both the mind and feelings. The Air Imbalance makes you think and worry constantly. The Water Imbalance makes you feel as if you are on an emotional roller coaster, but often you simply cause yourself extra anxiety; regardless of whatever you feel, you remain worried, unsure, sad, or perhaps depressed. Thus, you might worry over every detail, or you might find yourself extremely busy helping other people through their troubled times yet still have little satisfaction in your life. It is hard to be satisfied when your feelings constantly pull you toward moodiness and sadness. It is likely quite challenging to feel good about yourself, because the Water Imbalance keeps your emotions on a teeter-totter. Further, you likely have little or no sense of stability and contentment. Regardless of how the rest of your life is going, you are seldom satisfied.

The next step, then, is to complete the Earth Missions and Meditations. Once you begin to integrate Earth characteristics into your life, you will slow down some of these emotional and thought processes. As a result, you will find it easier to release some of your worry, because you will feel more centered and calm. Thus, first, we integrate some Earth grounding and centering before we begin to work on the Air and Water Imbalances.

Once you have found a greater sense of peace, I will ask you to work through all of the Missions and Meditations for both Air and Water. With other Imbalances, you would use the Meditations of one to offset the Imbalance of its polar opposite. However, since this Imbalance is of polar opposites, let us simply begin the work of focusing and integrating the positive aspects of each of these Elements into your life.

This Imbalance Combination will consistently create scenarios where you over think and feel strongly about almost everything. The Missions and Meditations will bring up issues for you, and you might be surprised at the strength of your reactions to them. I encourage you to keep coming back to that "Grounding" Meditation, and keep finding that sense of center and stability in the midst of whatever else is happening. From this more centered place, you will be able to make lasting changes in your own emotional and thinking patterns.

You might find you have a difficult time starting these Missions and Meditations. The Air part of your nature will want to take things in order, one at a time, and the Water part will want to jump around and choose intuitively. This seeming contradiction can make it challenging just to begin. To ease this transition, I ask you to honor both aspects of your nature by doing some of the Missions in order, and some randomly—to complete all of the Water Missions in order, and complete the Air Missions randomly. I am specifically asking you to complete the more analytical Missions randomly and the more intuitive Missions in an orderly manner. This will give you a chance to integrate both aspects a bit better.

When you have completed both the Air and Water Missions and Meditations, you will want to reassess yourself using the EDAT and EIAT. Evaluate your progress with respect to Element Designations and Imbalances. If you have no Imbalances, then you can feel free to move on to the next phase of the Element Integration Process. If you still have any Imbalances, please go back to the Missions and Meditations for Air and/or Water, and keep your focus on the positive aspects of each of these Elements during the process. Please note: This is not an overnight process. It will take some time to create and incorporate new patterns of feeling and thought. I encourage you to accept where you are right now without judgment, and then move forward from here.

However, do not be surprised if your second EDAT score yields multiple Element Designations (and also eventually decreases your Imbalance scores to zero). Remember, we want to imbue ourselves with all of their positive aspects, so this is a desirable outcome. When you begin to integrate the Elements through the

Missions and Meditations, you take on more of their characteristics, and more of them are available to you in beneficial ways. In the meantime, you will release some of your anxiety and some of your mood swings as you deepen and balance your connection to the positive aspects of both Air and Water.

With the next step, you will seek your active self. Complete the Fire Missions and Meditations. This last part of the Integration Process will help you feel more complete, whole, and passionately alive. You will then be free and open to live your life on your own terms, secure in the knowledge that you have a stable foundation, emotional health, creative passion, and mindfulness.

When you have completed all of the Missions and Meditations, assess your Designation one last time. Ideally, you will want to have scored so all four Elements are present in your EDAT. If any are not present, you will want to return to those Elements' Missions and Meditations and complete them again as you focus on their most positive aspects. Increasingly, you will find you are more able to identify the Elements working in your life. Once you have fully developed each of the Elements, please go to Chapters 19 and 20. Read through how to incorporate the Elements into your daily life, and then complete the "Meditation to Honor Your Completion of the Integration Process." This last part of the Integration Process will help you feel more complete and whole.

How do you proceed?

- To find peace and grounding before you proceed, go to the Earth Meditation: "Grounding" on page 185.
- To honor your positive Air Element characteristics, go to page 155 to complete the "Guided Meditation to the Air Element."
- To begin to address the Air Imbalance with Water Missions and Meditations, go to page 211.
- To honor your positive Water Element characteristics, please go to page 164 to complete the "Guided Meditation to the Water Element."
- To begin to address your Water Imbalance with Air Missions and Meditations, go to page 173.

- To reassess your Elements, go to the EDAT on page 48 or the EIAT on page 83.

Air/Earth Imbalance Description

Just like an Air Designation personality, someone with an Air Imbalance is also intelligence and thought-oriented. However, the Imbalance creates a personality more inclined to brood over issues, especially those over which the person has no control. The Earth Imbalance compounds this tendency to brood, because the Earth Imbalance person finds him or herself much more sedentary than he or she might otherwise be. These two tendencies work together to create an atmosphere rife for over thinking whatever issues are present. The trouble might stem from the fact that the Air/Earth Imbalance person has insufficient awareness of exactly what she or he is feeling. This person likely knows there are some deep emotions roiling internally, but has no method by which to acknowledge and deal with them. To compound matters, the person might blame him or herself for not doing something to change the current situation. These both occur because both the Air and Earth characteristics are out of balance, and therefore Water and Fire are less prevalent. Thus, it becomes extremely difficult either to feel your feelings or act on them appropriately. These two possibilities would be more present with an influx of Water and Fire energies, and therefore this is one of the things that must happen first.

To stop brooding over what happened, an Air/Earth Imbalance person must acknowledge his or her feelings about whatever caused the brooding episode. Despite the fact that it can be extremely challenging to beat the over thinking inertia an Air/Earth Imbalance can create, examining and acknowledging how one feels in the current situation (in other words, bringing Water into it) can help release the brooding and bring things to a more resolvable place.

Another issue an Earth/Air Imbalance person might encounter quite often is a real challenge in making decisions. The Air qualities will produce a desire to look at every facet of a situation, and an Air Imbalance will make that imperative. The Air person dearly needs to see and study every potential aspect of any situation. There is comfort to be found in the study of the situation, in part because no decisions have to be made immediately. Meanwhile, the Earth person has a stable and centered approach. The Earth Imbalance person takes this to an extreme in that the need for stability might make him or her too conservative, and perhaps inflexible. She or he might be unwilling or unable to take risks, no matter how small or potentially beneficial those risks might be. With this Combination, reaching a decision and acting on it might become almost impossible, because both Imbalances will keep the person from making and acting on decisions. In this case, Water's emotional awareness must be brought into play to mitigate the Air Imbalance, and Fire's ability and desire to act must mitigate the Earth Imbalance. Once the person has gained an awareness of his or her true feelings about the situation, and once she or he has developed a plan of action based on this awareness, Fire energy must be brought to act upon whatever decisions have been reached.

In simple terms, once you start thinking about something, you will gnaw away at it. You will spend time, days, weeks even, and do nothing but brood on whatever is bothering you. You might not have the emotional awareness to know the extent to which you are upset or hurt by whatever occurred. You will simply sit and stew in your own juices, as they say. The Earth Imbalance part of you (the part that lacks motivation to move forward and actively resolve whatever issues are present) will not allow action to take place, so you might feel paralyzed.

Mitigating an Air/Earth Imbalance

A significant part of stabilizing this particular Imbalance is to awaken your own conscious emotional awareness. Thus, the first thing to do to mitigate an Air/Earth Imbalance is to curtail the Air Imbalance-fueled tendencies to overanalyze, worry, and brood. Often, we spend time brooding over and analyzing issues because we are attempting to sweep our real feelings under the rug. We analyze things from various perspectives. We look at every possible facet of our current situation. The one thing we tend *not* to do is spend any time figuring out exactly how we feel. We bury our emotions in favor of well-reasoned arguments. In this way, it becomes easier to think about what has happened or might happen, rather than to accept how we feel about what is happening now.

Thus, the beginning of mitigating an Air/Earth Imbalance is to cultivate the emotional awareness of Water. Once we begin to access our emotions, we can then "check in" with ourselves to see how we truly feel about any given situation, and then make appropriate decisions that include our feelings as well as our thoughts. When we can acknowledge how we feel, we also bring to bear an incontrovertible truth; truly acknowledging our feelings about something will spur us to some kind of action or reaction, even if that reaction is simply the peaceful acknowledgement of what has occurred. This serves to help begin mitigating the Earth Imbalance as well.

You will want to access your feelings by working through all of the Water Missions and Meditations. Note your feelings as they occur. Initially, it might be difficult to see them when they occur, and it might also be difficult to be aware enough to note them and really feel them. I encourage you to keep trying. You will find it becomes easier each time you do it. Be sure to keep your thoughts and any feelings about your process in your Life Elements Journal, so you can gauge where you are and how far you have come.

After you complete the Water Missions and Meditations and have a better grasp of your feelings, you will want to offset your Earth Imbalance by cultivating some of Fire's passion, action, and creativity. These characteristics will help alleviate your affinity for shutting down and being static. The Missions and Meditations are designed to get you moving and to spark your creative spirit.

When you have completed both the Water and Fire Missions and Meditations, you will then want to reassess yourself using the EDAT and EIAT. Evaluate for yourself where you are with respect to Element Designations and Imbalances. You might be surprised to learn you have more Element Designations (and also lower Imbalance scores) since you have spent time cultivating additional Elements. As for your Air/Earth Imbalances, if you still have them, go to the Missions and Meditations section. However, this time, focus on and complete the Missions and Meditations for Earth and Air. This will give you access to the positive aspects of these two Elements, even as their characteristics are tempered by your newfound strength in Water and Fire. In the meantime, you will release some of your anxiety and isolation as you deepen your connection to the positive aspects of both Air and Earth.

Please note: This is not an overnight process. It will take some time to create and incorporate new patterns of stillness and thought. I encourage you to accept where you are right now without judgment, and then move forward from here. Do not be surprised if your second EDAT score yields multiple Element Designations (and also eventually decreases your Imbalance scores to zero). When you begin to integrate the Elements through the Missions and Meditations, you take on more of their characteristics, and more of them are available to you in beneficial ways. Remember, we want to imbue ourselves with all of their positive aspects, so this is a desirable outcome.

When you have completed all of the Missions and Meditations, assess your Designation once last time. Ideally, you will want to have scored so all four Elements are present in your EDAT. If any are not present, return to those Elements' Missions and Meditations and complete them again as you focus on their most positive aspects.

Increasingly, you will find you are more able to identify the Elements working in your life. Once you have fully developed each of the Elements, please go to Chapters 19 and 20. Read through how to incorporate the Elements into your daily life, and then complete the "Meditation to Honor Your Completion of the Integration Process." This last part of the Integration Process will help you feel more complete and whole. You will then be free and open to live your life on your own terms, secure in the knowledge you have a stable foundation, emotional health, creative passion, and mindfulness.

How do you proceed?

- To begin to address the Air Imbalance with Water Missions and Meditations, go to page 211.
- To begin to address your Earth Imbalance with Fire Missions and Meditations, go to page 199.
- To complete the Air Missions and Meditations, go to page 173.

- To complete the Earth Missions and Meditations, go to page 185.
- To reassess your Elements, go to the EDAT on page 48 or the EIAT on page 83.

Fire/Water Imbalance Description

A Fire/Water Designation person already lives in the state in which emotions rule and actions are taken quickly and sometimes rashly. A Fire/Water Imbalance takes this predilection to the next level. This "leap before you look because your feelings told you to do so" pattern can be problematic at the best of times. Unfortunately, a Fire/Water Imbalance lacks the Air characteristics that encourage thoughtful deliberation and the peaceful state of mind that allows for clear decision-making. It must be incredibly frustrating to have to deal with seldom feeling in calm control of the various situations in your life. It must feel as if control and peace are just around the corner, if only you take this one action. In other words, it might feel like there will be happiness if only this *next thing* is done, so it feels imperative to jump in, commit, and do whatever it is your feelings are telling you to do.

It must be extremely challenging to rein in those impulses to act, because Fire's passions drive the actions and Water's overly emotional state makes it difficult to stop, think, and plan. The consequence of this: when the hubbub has died down, the Fire/Water Imbalance person can be left feeling defeated and deflated, because no matter what actions were taken, those very Imbalances make it hard to feel the satisfaction of a completed project or course of action. By their nature, Fire and Water Imbalances urge further and extreme motion and emotion. They seldom bring peace of mind or serenity. Instead, they bring agitation borne of an emotional whirlwind, and a passionate desire to act, to satisfy some craving that cannot be satisfied until some of Fire's Imbalance is banked.

Mitigating a Fire/Water Imbalance

The first thing to do to mitigate a Fire/Water Imbalance is to curtail the Fire Imbalance-fueled actions being taken. In other words, we must minimize the consequences of actions taken due to the Fire Imbalance. Since Fire is the action Element, its influence is what urges us to act, and act right now, regardless of whether we have thought through what must be done. A Fire/Water Imbalance throws an emotional charge into the mix, and some people with a Fire/Water Imbalance find themselves overdoing and also having wide mood swings about the current situation, even as they attempt to do too much to resolve the issue. Thus, to begin to alleviate the Imbalance, we must first curb this immediate urge to do something, anything. We must find some stability and calm in the midst of whatever situations we find ourselves.

A significant part of stabilizing this particular Imbalance is to steady and calm both the emotions and the body. The Water Imbalance makes you very sensitive and empathetic, and also easily hurt. The Fire Imbalance makes you act to try to fix things, but often you simply cause yourself extra grief; regardless of what you try, you remain emotionally vulnerable, sensitive, and uncertain. Thus, you might run around like the proverbial headless chicken, or you might find yourself extremely busy and overcommitted, trying to solve everyone else's issues and problems. Yet, you might still have little satisfaction in your own life; in fact, you might find yourself depressed. It is hard to be satisfied when your instincts constantly pull you onward, so you likely seldom congratulate yourself on a job well done. Even if you complete your tasks, you will likely have still spent a great deal of energy in doing so. Further, you likely have little or no sense of stability and contentment, because regardless of how the rest of your life is going, you are never content and always looking for what might be around the corner. When you throw the potential for depression into the mix, it is easy to see why this is the most volatile of the Imbalance Combinations.

Please note: I believe it is possible to mend this Imbalance and to live fully and contentedly. It is challenging, but certainly not impossible to find balance and centering as you alleviate these Imbalances. Once you begin to slow some of the internal and external processes, you will find it easier to release some of the emotional charge because you will feel more centered and calm. Thus, first, we ease the Fire Imbalance and then, we will deal with Water.

First, you will want to achieve at least a temporary sense of calm by completing the Earth Meditation: "Grounding" on page 185. This will give you some time to center yourself, gain perspective, and acknowledge your current circumstances. At this point, please complete the Earth Missions. The Earth Missions' focus on centering and stability will work to assuage your Fire Imbalance.

In addition, work through the Earth Missions in order. Your Water characteristics might pull you toward doing only some of them, or completing them out of order. Here, to bring some of Air's order and deliberation into the mix, I encourage you to do the Missions in order, and with full deliberation. Some of you might see your competitive streak come to life here, and you might wish to do the one that sounds the most challenging immediately. Certainly, that is one of the methods you might choose. However, sometimes jumping into the most challenging one might work, and sometimes it might backfire. If you jump into the most challenging Mission right away, you might find you might not complete it, or you will go "whole hog" as it were. Then, the very idea of calming the Fire Imbalance will be a bit muddied as your competitive, overly hectic nature will keep you from fully experiencing the stabilizing benefits of the Earth Missions.

When you establish a solid foundation in Earth Element characteristics, you will begin to notice you have a greater sense of peace and serenity. The sense of peace will not come immediately, but if you persevere, you will increasingly find you remain calmer and more content. (Incidentally, this will also help some of the emotional roller-coaster patterns of the Water Imbalance.) The urge to run from one thing to the next will begin to subside. When this occurs, there will be room to incorporate the positive aspects of your fiery nature. Earth Missions are incredibly helpful in mitigating a Fire Imbalance, precisely because they ask you to slow down and achieve a sense of peace.

Once you complete the Earth Missions and firmly establish an atmosphere conducive to alleviating the Fire Imbalance, you will want to begin to mitigate the Water Imbalance. Just as a Fire Imbalance is best fixed by Earth, its polar opposite, a Water Imbalance is best alleviated by using the positive aspects of Air.

When you have smoothed out some of the Water Imbalance with Air, you will then be able to integrate some of the positive aspects of mindfulness from a calm state.

Air governs thought, intelligence, reason, truth, and honesty. These are the very things you will want to bring into your life to help you see things differently: to find a sense of reasoned calm and mindful action. When you cultivate Air Element characteristics, you will enable yourself to find your path from a thoughtful place. The challenging moods that might so affect your life right now will cease to have such prominence. Right now, you are likely most inclined to be sensitive, moody, and wrenched by the slightest things. Despite the fact that it might be difficult, it will be of great benefit to you to step back as best you can so you can give some thought to your current state. This thoughtful state will help ease some of the emotional pressure you are under. It is opening the steam valve, as it were. You might have been experiencing too much stress and pressure, and you might be afraid there is no help or hope for resolving any of the emotion-laden issues that currently demand your attention. It is time to slow down and give mindful attention to what sits in front of you.

With thought and reason, you will begin to find your center and continue the process of Element Integration. I recognize it can feel impossible to make lasting changes, because the dramas in your life always seem to cause you grief. You might even feel like each new challenge is just too much to handle because you are so emotionally impacted by them. It might even feel like you have no choice in how your emotions make you react. However, my point here is that with Air's influence, you can create a pattern of thoughtful and deliberate assessment of your status. Then, with that thoughtful and reasoned perspective, your emotions can be expressed honestly and fully.

Ideally, once you have dealt with each of these Imbalances, you will have simultaneously brought the positive aspects of Earth and Air into your life. You already had strength in Fire and Water before you began this process; however, the Elements provided you with too many of their less-than-positive characteristics (hence the Imbalance). You then mitigated those characteristics by focusing on the positive aspects of Water and Fire's polar opposites. Now, you are ready to create an atmosphere of growth and integration. The next step in this process will be to address any lingering Imbalance issues, and to reassess with the EDAT and EIAT. Take note if you still receive any Element Imbalances. If you do receive Imbalances in either Fire or Water, go back to the Missions and Meditations section, but this time complete the Fire and Water Missions and Meditations. Take the time to focus on their most positive aspects as you complete the Missions.

Please note: This is not an overnight process. It will take some time to incorporate and create new patterns of feeling and behavior. I encourage you to accept where you are right now without judgment, and then move forward from here. Do not be surprised if your second EDAT score yields multiple Element Designations (and also eventually decreases your Imbalance scores to zero). When you begin to integrate the Elements through the Missions and Meditations, you take on more of their characteristics, and more of them are available to you in beneficial ways. Remember, we want to imbue ourselves with all of their positive aspects, so this is a desirable outcome.

When you have completed all the Missions and Meditations, assess your Designation one last time. Ideally, you will want to have scored so all four Elements are present in your EDAT. If any are not present, you will want to return to those Elements' Missions and Meditations and complete them again as you focus on their most positive aspects.

Increasingly, you will find you are more able to identify the Elements working in your life. Once you have fully developed each of the Elements, please go to Chapters 19 and 20. Read through how to incorporate the Elements into your daily life, and then complete the "Meditation to Honor Your Completion of the Integration Process." This last part of the Integration Process will help you feel more complete and whole. You will then be free and open to live your life on your own terms, secure in the knowledge you have a stable foundation, emotional health, creative passion, and mindfulness.

How do you proceed?

- To find peace and grounding before you proceed, go to the Earth Meditation: "Grounding" on page 185.
- To honor your positive Fire Element characteristics, please go to page 159 to complete the "Guided Meditation to the Fire Element."
- To begin to address the Fire Imbalance with Earth Missions, go to page 188.
- To honor your positive Water Element characteristics, please go to page 164 to complete the "Guided Meditation to the Water Element."
- To begin to address your Water Imbalance with Air Missions and Meditations, go to page 173.
- To reassess your Elements, go to the EDAT on page 48 or the EIAT on page 83.

Fire/Earth Imbalance Description

A person who has a Fire/Earth Imbalance can be in for some challenging times. The Fire Imbalance characteristics of running full-tilt and leaping before you look operate in conjunction with the Earth Imbalance propensities to be sedentary and potentially rigid. In other words, someone with this Combination Imbalance might find him or herself going to extremes of frenetic action, motion, and passion until something happens to stop the forward momentum. Then, she or he will sit and do nothing, become sedentary, and find it incredibly difficult to motivate him or herself to do anything until the next trigger for action occurs. This trigger often occurs from external sources such as friends or partners. The person with this Imbalance Combination will have a tough time motivating him or herself, but will have no trouble running out and staying out until quite late if she or he is in the pursuit of lovers or partnership. This will go on until something happens, once again, to curtail the forward motion. Then the other extreme comes into play and the person will sit at home, watch a lot of television (or play a lot of computer games) and have little contact with others. It almost appears as if this person is buffeted by the winds of fate. The two Imbalances and their characteristic counterparts tend to make it extremely challenging to approach situations from a centered place because such extremes of action/inaction are maintained.

Whereas a Fire/Earth Designation person might find a balance between being still and being in motion, a Fire/Earth Imbalance person has a much greater challenge in deciding whether moving forward is appropriate. The trouble stems from the fact that a Fire Imbalance encourages movement in most circumstances, regardless of whether it is the most beneficial thing to do. An Earth Imbalance promotes a sedentary, uncompromising attitude. When these two come together, the person might feel pulled to either act rashly or sit completely still, and often both at the same time. Thus, he or she might find him or herself either jumping the gun or waiting too long to do what actually needs to be done. Often, a Fire/Earth Imbalance person is either running around too much to see the correct path, or sitting too still to actually do something about getting on that path.

Neither Element Imbalance encourages action at an opportune moment. Thus, the person is left inactive and yet under a great deal of stress. This is because she or he believes nothing works, and so might think, "Why bother?" This "why bother" attitude becomes pervasive after a number of failed attempts. Without the thoughtful influence of Air or the ability to acknowledge how she or he really feels, the Earth/Fire Imbalance person operates uncertainly. She or he runs up many blind alleys, and finds no satisfaction until she or he stops trying all together. That is when the Earth Imbalance kicks in and makes it hard to motivate to try again, or to use the quiet time for reflection and meditative learning rather than simply sitting and watching television, for example.

Once the Fire/Earth Imbalance person has "given up," it is increasingly difficult to find motivation to move forward from a balanced place. The two Imbalances create a continuous cycle of overactivity that leads directly a great deal of underactivity. Unfortunately, because there seems to be little focused transition time between the two extremes, it can be very challenging for the person with this Imbalance to maintain equilibrium and act from a calm and focused place. This attainment of balance between stasis and hyper-action must be achieved to resolve the Imbalance.

Mitigating a Fire/Earth Imbalance

Just like an Air/Water Imbalance, a Fire/Earth Imbalance consists of a combination of polar opposites, a duality if you will. This is a more challenging Imbalance Combination to resolve, because while the other Imbalances can be resolved with the Elements that are naturally inclined to mitigate the Imbalance, in this case, the mitigating Elements are the ones out of balance. This can make the person with the Imbalance feel as if little is in his or her control. Things might feel off-kilter and too unstable.

Generally, when mitigating an Imbalance, we want to look at the polar opposite of the Element Imbalance we are attempting to alleviate. In this case, however, the two Imbalances are already polar opposites, since usually we would equalize an Earth Imbalance with Fire Missions and Meditations, and vice versa. Thus, any time there is an Imbalance of polar opposite Elements (Fire/Earth or Air/Water), this creates a particularly volatile set of characteristics. This means we must develop a new paradigm for dealing with the Imbalance.

Before that can occur, however, the person must acknowledge this Imbalance plays a role in his or her life. Once we name an issue in our lives, it becomes much easier to resolve it. The Earth/Fire Imbalance person brings to the table an incredible amount of energy to accomplish tasks. The Fire Imbalance portion of this takes all that energy and turns it into frenetic activity that sometimes has no actual goal. If there is a problem to be handled, for example, a Fire Imbalance person will jump in to begin to solve it without first giving thought to the best course of action. If she or he is lucky, one of the things she or he does will fix the problem. If not, then the frustration can skyrocket. Then, the Earth portion of this will begin to exert the idea that it is futile to keep trying, and things will begin to shut down. The person will become despondent that nothing worked, and will begin to feed into the idea that there is no way she or he can handle and successfully complete whatever it is that needs to be done, regardless of how much she or he tries. It is an insidious path because it feeds back upon itself, and the cycle continues.

As we have seen above, the Earth/Fire Imbalance vacillates between overactivity and underactivity. Either you are going nonstop, or you find it hard to get out of bed in the morning. There seems to be no middle ground, and that makes it much more challenging to change your patterns. It is difficult to make lasting, positive changes if life feels like a tilt-a-whirl that is either stopped or going full-tilt. In this case, we either give ourselves no time to think, or our thinking patterns become so lethargic, we can no longer envision that change might be possible. So, the first thing we need to do is begin to change some of our internal monologue. The internal monologue is best defined as the thoughts that run through us as we move through our day. They are not necessarily about what we must accomplish or whom we must see. They are the thoughts we think while we prepare to begin a new project or speak to someone new, or simply what we think in our own private moments. William James described it as a stream of consciousness.

The internal monologue is our tour guide through our day-to-day life. It keeps us company and talks us through everything we do. Here is the kicker: We would like to think that our Inner Tour Guide (ITG) is our biggest fan, our staunchest ally. Unfortunately, that is seldom the case. Most often, the ITG is caustic, sarcastic, and downright insulting. When we try to do something, the ITG tells us we will not succeed, or even more insidiously, it tells us not to bother even trying. In an Earth/Fire Imbalance, the ITG seems to keep up a constant barrage of "why bother?" thoughts. One of the ways the Earth/Fire Imbalance is maintained is that the ITG supports both the overactivity *and* the underactivity when each occurs. Our job here is to ensure that the ITG gets some new dialogue. We must give it new things to say so the pattern of negative self-talk is broken and we can create a greater distance between the periods of over and underactivity and establish more-helpful patterns in the times between those extremes.

One of the best ways to establish new patterns of positive self-talk and therefore begin to increase that in-between time is to give the ITG new dialogue. Here we will do that by turning to the Air Element and giving our ITG new words to think. I have found this is best established by something called *affirmations*. Shakti Gawain and Julia Cameron wrote eloquently about affirmations in their books, *Creative Visualizations* and *The Artist's Way* respectively.

Affirmations are positive, life-affirming statements we repeat to ourselves to change our internal thought patterns. If we give the ITG different things to say, we will likely find it becomes easier to maintain equilibrium in the face of our challenges.

Now, what is it we wish to accomplish? Right now, we want to establish the rules of the road for mitigating this Imbalance. First, we must establish a time period between the roller coaster of over and underactivity. We will find the moment that exists directly before one type starts and the other stops. Then, we will create space to access some of the other states of being that will make it easier to move forward from a balanced place.

First, read through the statements below. Some of these might feel relevant, and some might feel downright ridiculous because they appear to be so far from the truth. Regardless of how relevant they currently feel, I will ask you to close your eyes, believe if only for a moment, and think these thoughts as if following statements are true in your life right now.

"I am serene and content."

"I am able to act when the time is right, and I am able to be still when the time is right."

"I can find peace and joy in focused stillness and motion."

"I deserve happiness and fulfillment."

"I am entitled to conscious delight, peace, and relaxation."

"I work diligently, and I also find time for joyful play."

"I create the peaceful life I want every day, and I find pleasure in thoughtful forward motion."

"I consider my options carefully before I reach decisions, and then I act on those decisions calmly."

Let us consider the above statements for a moment. Did any of them elicit a reaction of some sort? Please write down your initial reaction to each in your Life Elements Journal; it is a good idea to note how you feel right now.

Find a blank page in your Life Elements Journal. The first statement—"I am serene and content"—seems straightforward, even if you feel neither serene nor content. Please write the statement five times, and take a deep breath between each time. Assess how you feel after having done so, and write down your reactions. This is challenging, yet it is also important, since it will give you insight into some of the reasons for the Element Imbalance.

Now, continue to write each of the statements five times. As you write, take a moment and really think through what they mean to you, and what reaction they elicit as you write them. Eventually, you might find rewording the statements makes them more relevant. For right now, however, please work with the wordings I have written. Doing so will give you invaluable aid in finding that focused stillness before conscious action. The very action of taking the time to write them will help because while it is action, it is *focused* action. You are not just being sedentary, yet you are not running hither and yon. You are instead taking time to be thoughtful before you proceed with your day. This is the beginning.

It is hard to make lasting, positive changes if there is no stable base on which to build. Once you have carved out some of that mindful space, you will need to find a sense of calm and serenity. The best way to calm your Fire nature is to incorporate some positive Earth Element energy into your life. Specifically, Earth energy brings awareness, centering, and serenity to you. That becomes necessary in going through any step-by-step process to make changes you both want to make and feel strong enough to make. When you establish a solid foundation in positive Earth Element characteristics, you will begin to notice you have a greater sense of peace and serenity. The sense of peace will not come immediately, but if you persevere, you will find, more and more, that increasingly you remain calmer and more content. This will give you some of that in-between time to begin accessing more of the positive aspects of Earth and Fire.

Once you have found a greater sense of in-between time, I ask you to work through all the Missions and Meditations for both Earth and Fire. With other Imbalances, you would use the Missions of one to offset the Imbalance of its polar opposite. However, since this Imbalance consists of polar opposites, let us simply begin the work of integrating the positive aspects of each of these Elements into your life. This Imbalance Combination will consistently create cycles where you overdo, and then become sedentary and do nothing at all. The Missions and Meditations will bring up issues for you, and you might be surprised at the strength of your reactions to them. I encourage you to keep coming back to the Air Affirmations above. Keep finding that sense of space between frenetic activity and complete inactivity in the midst of whatever else is happening. Keep finding the sense of thoughtful space that comes from spending time simply writing these sentences. From this more mindful place, you will be able to make lasting changes to become more conscious about when it is time to be still, and when it is time to act.

When you have completed both the Earth and Fire Missions and Meditations, you will want to reassess yourself using the EDAT and EIAT. Evaluate for yourself where you are now with respect to Element Designations and Imbalances. If you still have any Imbalances, go back to the Missions and Meditations for Earth and/ or Fire and keep working through the Missions for both of them. Please note: This is not an overnight process. It will take some time to create and incorporate new patterns of stillness and motion. I encourage you to accept where you are right now without judgment, and then move forward from here.

In the next step, you will continue your cultivation of the Elements. You will find your thoughtful, analytical self by exploring the Air Missions and Meditations. Complete each of them to broaden your access to Air characteristics. Then, you will discover your emotional self by completing the Water Missions and Meditations. You will seek and find your heart center. Then, reassess with the EDAT and EIAT. Do not be surprised if this EDAT score yields multiple Element Designations (and also eventually decreases your Imbalance scores to zero). When you begin to integrate the Elements through the Missions and Meditations, you take on more of their characteristics, and more of them are available to you in beneficial ways. Remember, we want to imbue ourselves with all of their positive aspects, so this is a desirable outcome.

When you have completed all of the Missions and Meditations, assess your Designation one last time. Ideally, you will want to have scored so that all four Elements are present in your EDAT. If any are not present, you will want to return to those Elements' Missions and Meditations and complete them again as you focus on their most positive aspects.

Increasingly, you will find you are more able to identify the Elements working in your life. Once you have fully developed each of the Elements, please go to Chapters 19 and 20. Read through how to incorporate the Elements into your daily life, and then complete the "Meditation to Honor Your Completion of the Integration Process." This last part of the Integration Process will help you feel more complete and whole. You will then be free and open to live your life on your own terms, secure in the knowledge that you have a stable foundation, emotional health, creative passion, and mindfulness.

How do you proceed?

- To find the Earth Missions and Meditations, go to page 185.
- To find Fire Missions and Meditations, go to page 199.
- To find Air Missions and Meditations, go to page 173.
- To find Water Missions and Meditations, go to page 211.
- To reassess your Elements, go to the EDAT on page 48 or the EIAT on page 83.

Water/Earth Imbalance Description

People with Water/Earth Imbalance Combination might find they suffer from depression. The feeling of being adrift, even while in your own home, might be somewhat familiar to you. You might feel as if you have trouble finding a place that is yours and where you belong. You might feel as if you have no stable center even though you are a homebody, and you might feel lost unless someone else gives you stability or something to hold on to.

The Water/Earth Imbalance happens more often than many of us realize. The hyperemotional traits of a Water Imbalance and immobility of an Earth Imbalance can combine to create a sense of hopelessness in the person with this Combination Imbalance. An attitude of the futility of things can prevail because the sad or depressive emotions work on the sedentary state and make it dip into a potentially debilitating depression.

It is not surprising when Water/Earth Imbalance people find themselves in a state of paralysis about life issues. However, there is a center to fall back on here, because there are some Earth Element characteristics that allow for the center to be available sometimes.

The catch here is that this center tends to focus on the "why bother?" aspects of things. Rather than seeing the current depressed state as temporary, Earth/Water Imbalance people see it as permanent and unchangeable, and tend to focus on only its negative aspects. "If everything is permanent and unchangeable, then why bother trying to fix it?" tends to be the attitude. Then, the more negative emotions take the stage. Or, if the Water Imbalance has taken the form of wide mood swings, then hopes are built up high and the people have grandiose ideas/hopes, yet the Earth Imbalance somehow keeps them from ever acting on those plans.

Then, there is an added issue, in that the Water Imbalance and its tendency toward negativity bring self-deprecation and guilt. This gives the person yet another reason to stay hidden and paralyzed, and keeps him or her from acting and perhaps improving the situation. Rather than seeing the center and home space as a starting point, the Water/Earth Imbalance person tends to see it as the end, and maintains the attitude that nothing changes anyway.

Mitigating a Water/Earth Imbalance

The way to mitigate a Water/Earth Imbalance is to find that stable center and gain emotional stability from there. We must access a stable foundation to move forward. It is important to minimize the occurrence of situations where the Earth/Water Imbalance person spirals into feelings of sadness, depression, and hopelessness, and then stays there because of the Earth Imbalance tendency to remain static.

A significant part of stabilizing this particular Imbalance is to cultivate an emotional center and a home base that feels safe and stable. The center already exists to an extent; however, it focuses on the negative aspects of isolation and solitude. Instead, of being focused on the peace that can come from centering, the attitude tends to revert to, "It's not worth it, so I'm not going to do anything at all." So, there needs to be a paradigm shift to a slightly more proactive and positive approach to center. One of the best ways to do this is to begin to find a sense of calm and serenity in your current state.

There is an ancient proverb attributed to either Buddha or Confucius (et. al.), and it states: "Wherever you go, there you are." Popularized in the 1984 movie, *The Adventures of Buckaroo Banzai Across the 8th Dimension*, this bit of advice is one of the first things that might begin to resolve and release this Imbalance. Earth Imbalance people tend to accept the present circumstances, and then believe that regardless of the quality of what is going on, any negative aspects are simply par for the course. Then, the Water Imbalance makes them feel badly, but the Earth Imbalance keeps them from acting to improve things in any way. Plus, the Water Imbalance keeps hopes high for every new potential solution, and then if it does not work, the hopes are dashed, and the Earth Imbalance makes it challenging to try any other options.

There are multiple layers here, and they all feed on one another to continue the cycle. So, before anything else happens, we must work on acceptance of the current situation. The key here is that it needs to be acceptance without judgment. We can accept where we sit and be frustrated that it is not better, or we can accept our situation and then realize it is simply a transitory state. Things will change and move. They will never stay completely the same. This means that regardless of how you feel and perhaps how much you beat yourself up about your current circumstances, they will change. Your Mission in this scenario is to accept the current state, and if possible, release your guilt about it.

One of the things I have noticed in my life coaching practice is that guilt rarely yields beneficial results. Guilt serves to paralyze, or if it spurs us into action, the action is furtive and not well planned. So, I will encourage you here to begin to accept where you are. It is time to accept your center as an okay place to be. I want to encourage you to stop judging yourself harshly. Water/Earth Imbalance people tend to beat themselves up about their circumstances, because not only do they believe themselves helpless and stuck, but they also feel badly and guilty about it on top of everything else. This does you no good. You will want to find a calm center, and then release some of that negative emotion. As I say to my clients, you need to open the steam valve a bit.

Before you can seek that stable center, however, you have to find that spark that will motivate you to make a change in the first place. That spark can be found in the active characteristics of Fire.

Once you have sparked yourself to begin, you will find it increasingly easier to walk your path to your center. So, here I will ask you to complete the Fire Kahuna Fire walker Meditation on page 159. This Meditation will help give you some passion for the doing of things, and thus help you start the journey.

Once you have completed the Kahuna Meditation, you will begin to address the Water and Earth Imbalances. The Water Imbalance makes you overly-sensitive and empathetic, and also easily hurt. The Earth Imbalance makes you pull into yourself, and yet remain uncertain of your own worth. Thus, you might feel both depressed and hopeless simultaneously. You might believe there are no solutions, because neither your Earth nor Water Imbalance leaves you room to explore with Air's reasoning or Fire's forward motion. Further, you likely have little or no sense of stability and contentment, because regardless of how the rest of your life is going, you are seldom satisfied. This dissatisfaction occurs because your Water Imbalance predisposes you to look at the world through less than optimistic perspectives. When you throw into the mix the potential for remaining static, it is easy to see how you might spiral down into depressive episodes. You might feel like Eeyore from *Winnie the Pooh*. You are likely both sad, and have the feeling that you have no real, stable base to get help.

Please note: I fully believe it is possible to mend these Imbalances to live fully and contentedly. It is challenging, but certainly not impossible to find balance and centering as you integrate the Elements. The way to proceed from here is to continue to increase your ability to act when the time is right. Water and Earth will pull you toward closing in and shutting down, and if you cultivate Fire, you will be building a resistance to those urges. Instead, you will be incorporating more activity into your life. This activity will be the building block of other, more significant changes later.

Here, you will want to complete the rest of the Fire Missions and Meditations to address the Earth Imbalance. I encourage you to maintain a regimen of doing some of them at least once a week, until doing them becomes second nature to you. This will create an atmosphere of forward motion, and will move you into a greater freedom to act when the time is right.

Once you have worked through and become comfortable completing the Fire Missions and Meditations, you will want to bring some of Air's order and deliberation into the mix. Just as an Earth Imbalance is best addressed by its polar opposite, Fire, a Water Imbalance is best alleviated by using the positive aspects of Air. Air governs thought, intelligence, reason, truth, and honesty. These are the very things you will want to bring into your life to help you see things differently, and to find a sense of reasoned calm and mindful action. When you cultivate Air Element characteristics, you will enable yourself to find your path from a mindful place. The challenging moods that might so affect your life right now will cease to have such prominence.

Right now, you are likely most inclined to be sensitive and moody, and wrenched by the slightest things. Despite the fact it might be difficult, it will be of great benefit to you to step back as best you can so you can give some thought to your current state. This thoughtful state will help ease some of the emotional pressure you are under. It is opening the steam valve, as it were. You might have been experiencing too much stress and pressure, and you might be afraid there is no help or hope for resolving any of the emotion-laden issues that currently demand your attention. It is time to slow down and give mindful attention to what sits in front of you. With thoughtfulness, you will begin to find your center and complete the process of Element Integration.

Please note: I recognize it can feel impossible to make lasting changes, because events in your life always seem to cause you grief. You might even feel like each new challenge is just too much to handle because you are so emotionally affected by it. However, I must stress, it is indeed possible to make those lasting changes and to ease the dramas in your life.

I suggest you try to do the Air Missions in order, and with deliberation. You will eventually want to complete all of the Air Missions and Meditations to achieve the mindfulness Air characteristics can give you. When you establish an atmosphere of mindfulness through Air Element characteristics, you will begin to notice you have a greater sense of deliberate motion in your life. You will no longer feel such a need to close in and shut down, and instead you will begin to approach issues from a place of reasoned action. The sense of reasoned action will not come immediately, but if you persevere, you will increasingly find that you remain more mindful, and when you act, you will do so from a thoughtful place. The urge to shut down will begin to subside, and when this occurs, there will be room to incorporate the positive aspects of your solid and emotion-filled nature.

I encourage you to move forward deliberately and thoughtfully so your emotions do not overtake your desire to proceed. Your basic Water nature might tug you away from the deliberate work that needs to be done. You will want to complete each Mission thoughtfully, and with feelings of calm deliberation, so as not to disturb your already fragile emotional state. To do so, take the time to breathe deeply and evenly for at least one minute before you begin any of the Missions or Meditations. The focused breathing and Air's sense of analysis and mindfulness can be incredibly helpful in mitigating a Water Imbalance.

When you have smoothed out some of the Water Imbalance with Air, you will then be able to integrate some positive aspects of mindfulness from a place of calm. Ideally, once you have dealt with each of these Imbalances, you will have brought the positive aspects of both Air and Fire into your life. You already had strength in Earth and Water before you began this process; however, these Elements provided you with too many of their less-than-positive characteristics. You then mitigated those characteristics by focusing on the positive aspects of Earth and Water's polar opposites.

The next step in this process will be to address any lingering Earth/Water Imbalance issues with a reevaluation of the EDAT and EIAT. Assess your Designations and any Imbalances by completing the EDAT and EIAT again. Take note if you still receive any Element Imbalances. If so, you will want to return to the Missions and Meditations. This time, however, focus on the Missions and Meditations for Earth and Water. This will give you access to the positive aspects of these two Elements, even as their characteristics are tempered by your newfound strength in Fire and Air.

When you begin the Earth Missions and Meditations, first go through the Earth Meditation: "Grounding" on page 185. Then, I will ask you to repeat this ground-and-center Meditation as often as possible, until you feel connected to that which is around you. Once you begin to feel connected, I think you will slowly begin to believe you are a valuable part of everything. This will promote the positive aspects of Earth.

Before you complete the Water Missions and Meditations, you will need to come to terms with some of your negative emotions. We tend to get into a downward spiral of bad feeling and self-judgment. We feel badly, and then we judge ourselves harshly for our bad feelings. In the David Mamet movie, *House of Games*, one of the characters says: "When you have done something unforgivable, forgive yourself." In many ways, this is true. To many, something that is unforgivable is a daily occurrence for others. Some judge themselves, and some do not. Guilt plays a role here, and I ask you to think about the role acceptance might play.

Are there ways in which you can accept your current state wherever it happens to be? If so, then this acceptance can be the next step on your healing journey. Here, I encourage you to say the words, "I accept myself, here and now." Right now, close your eyes, sit back comfortably, and say those words to yourself five times. Really make the attempt to feel acceptance. Take a deep breath, and as you do so, say those words. As you exhale, try to feel accepted. Try it now.

Did it feel strange or uncomfortable? If it did, then I encourage you to keep trying it, every day. Your Water Imbalance will keep you feeling off-kilter until you take it in hand and make sure your emotions no longer control you. It is too easy for you to feel like you are at the whims of your feelings. It does not have to be this way. You can choose. You can decide how much ill feeling or mood-swinging will go on in your life, and this is the beginning of making those decisions.

Please note: This is not an overnight process. It will take some time to incorporate and create new patterns of feeling and stability. I encourage you to accept where you are right now without judgment, and then move forward from here. Do not be surprised if your second EDAT score yields multiple Element Designations (and also eventually decreases your Imbalance scores to zero).

When you begin to integrate the Elements through the Missions and Meditations, you take on more of their characteristics, and more of them are available to you in beneficial ways. Remember, we want to imbue ourselves with all of their positive aspects, so this is a desirable outcome.

When you have completed all of the Missions and Meditations, assess your Designation one last time. Ideally, you will want to have scored so all four Elements are present in your EDAT. If there any are not present, you will want to return to those Elements' Missions and Meditations and complete them again as you focus on their most positive aspects.

Increasingly, you will find you are more able to identify the Elements working in your life. Once you have fully developed each of the Elements, please go to Chapters 19 and 20. Read through how to incorporate the Elements into your daily life, and then complete the "Meditation to Honor Your Completion of the Integration Process." This last part of the Integration Process will help you feel more complete and whole. You will then be free and open to live your life on your own terms, secure in the knowledge that you have a stable foundation, emotional health, creative passion, and mindfulness.

How do you proceed?

- To find the spark of motivation to proceed, go to the "Guided Meditation to the Fire Element" (Fire Kahuna Meditation) on page 159.
- To find the Earth Meditation: "Grounding," go to page 185.
- To begin to address the Earth Imbalance with Fire Missions and Meditations, go to page 199.
- To begin to address the Water Imbalance with Air Missions and Meditations, go to page 173.
- To reassess your Elements, go to the EDAT on page 48 or the EIAT on page 83.

Chapter 12
What Is the Order of Events?

Some of you who have read this far might feel a bit overwhelmed at the number of steps involved in this process. To put you at ease, below are the steps to follow.

The Steps on the Path to Elemental Integration

1. Complete your Element Designation and Imbalance assessments.
2. Honor the Element(s) you are right now.
3. Address any Element Imbalances by completing the appropriate included Missions and Meditations.
4. Cultivate the other Elements to bring yourself into integration with Earth, Air, Fire, and Water.
5. Determine the ways in which you might incorporate the Elements into your daily life.
6. Complete the "Meditation to Honor Your Completion of the Integration Process." Once the characteristics of all four Elements are accessible to you, you will have the stability and center of Earth, the thoughtfulness and mindfulness of Air, the emotional awareness of Water, and the passions and action of Fire. You will then be free to explore the rest of your life from this joyful integrated perspective.
7. Live a GREAT life!

Here is a more detailed picture of the steps involved when you are addressing Imbalances or integrating the four Elements. Please note: If you have Imbalances, please address them before completing the rest of the Integration Process.

Complete the Missions and Meditations in the following order when you have no Imbalances and a single Element Designation:

Single Element Designation (No Imbalances)	Order in which to complete Missions and Meditations
Earth	Air, Water, Fire
Air	Fire, Earth, Water
Fire	Air, Water, Earth
Water	Fire, Earth, Air

Complete the Missions and Meditations in the following order when you have no Imbalances and a Combination Element Designation:

Element Combination (No Imbalances)	Order in which to complete Meditations and Missions
Air (dominant)/Fire	Fire, Earth, Water
Fire (dominant)/Air	Air, Water, Earth
Air (dominant)/Water	Water, Earth, Fire
Water (dominant)/Air	Air, Fire, Earth
Air (dominant)/Earth	Earth, Fire, Water
Earth (dominant)/Air	Air, Water, Fire
Water (dominant)/Fire	Fire, Earth, Air
Fire (dominant)/Water	Water, Air, Earth
Earth (dominant)/Fire	Fire, Air, Water
Fire (dominant)/Earth	Earth, Air, Water
Water (dominant)/Earth	Earth, Fire, Air
Earth (dominant)/Water	Water, Air, Fire

Complete the Missions and Meditations in the following order when you have a single Element Imbalance.

Single Element Imbalance	Initial Guided Meditation	Order for completing Missions and Meditations
Earth	Earth, pg. 185	Fire, Air, Water, Earth
Air	Air, pg. 155	Water, Fire, Earth, Air
Fire	Fire, pg. 160	Earth, Air, Water, Fire

Single Element Imbalance	Initial Guided Meditation	Order for completing Missions and Meditations
Water	Water, pg. 164	Air, Earth, Fire, Water

Complete the Missions and Meditations in the following order when you have a Combination Element Imbalance.

Combination Element Imbalance	Initial Meditation or Activity	Order in which to complete Missions and Meditations
Air/Fire	Earth Guided, pg. 185	Earth, Water, Air, Fire
Air/Water	Earth Guided, pg. 185	Earth, Air, Water, Fire
Air/Earth	Water Guided, pg. 164	Water, Fire, Air, Earth
Fire/Water	Earth Guided, pg. 185	Earth, Air, Fire, Water
Fire/Earth	Air Activity, pg. 132	Earth, Fire, Air, Water
Water/Earth	Fire Guided, pg. 160	Fire, Air, Water, Earth

Element Designation Recap

First, ascertain your Element Designation(s) and your strengths in each of the Elements. Then, ascertain your Imbalances in any Elements and address any Imbalances. (Go to the Element Imbalance instructions to see how to proceed if you need to address Imbalances.) Honor your designated Element by completing the guided meditation to that Element.

You are already strong in your designated Element—you just need to be aware of it, and perhaps guard against moving too much into the Element—so other than keeping yourself aware of your natural inclinations in responses to stimuli, you do not have to do much in that Element. Now, you need to begin from wherever you are in your particular Elemental Round-Robin. Once you know where you are, you can then move along the grids above to complete the Integration Process.

Element Imbalance At-a-Glance

Addressing an Imbalance is bit more challenging. Each Element has a mirror opposite on the medicine wheel. If you look at the figure below, the wheel can be divided into four parts. Earth and Fire are on opposite sides, and Air and Water are on opposite sides.

Figure 1.   This diagram illustrates the positions of the Elements on the medicine wheel. Note the polar opposite locations of Earth and Fire and also Water and Air.

The Elements on opposite sides are related to one another and balance one another. When someone has issues descriptive of a Water Imbalance, for example, it can be described in terms of a function of Air. So, someone who has issues with extreme mood swings might be unable to internally reason out the current circumstances. Another example occurs if someone has issues of not being able to sit still. If, in fact, she or he can never commit to anything or maintain a healthy longer-term relationship, or even simply spend any time in peaceful repose, then it can be said that she or he has too much Fire in her or his personality, or the Earth Element is not mitigating the Fire Element sufficiently, and therefore there is a Fire Imbalance.

Conversely, if a person is too sedentary and therefore does not act when it is appropriate to do so, if she or he or finds him or herself solely watching television, not having any hobbies, or not going out and maintaining a social life, then it can be said she or he has an Earth Imbalance. Some of Fire's impetus can be used to mitigate the sedentary Earth Imbalance. The same can be said for Air and Water. Too much influence of one Element can bring about an Imbalance in its polar opposite.

Since the most optimal way is to balance all four and to have their characteristics and strengths available to you when you need them, we must work to ensure that balance is reached between them. Therefore, we treat an overabundance of one by accessing its polar opposite.

What Are You Thinking?

You might need or wish to take some time and assess for yourself the extent to which you agree with the EDAT and EIAT assessments. One of the ways to do that is to determine your level of comfort with the Elements themselves. The next chapter is designed to give you an introduction to the Elements individually—not as descriptions of personality types, but more as visualizations that will guide you to the imaginary realms of the Elements themselves. By going to visit each one, you will see your own state and responses mirrored in your reaction to completing these Guided Meditations. Do each one, and assess your response for yourself. Pay attention to your comfort level, and to any specific reactions. If you find that one or more of them make you uncomfortable, note for yourself what it is that makes you feel this way. It might be that you simply dislike water or being in the water, for example. And this might be a historic thing with you.

However, I submit for your consideration that it is possible that the very reason you have issues with water might be that the Water Element has somehow played a significant role in your life. It is therefore even more necessary for you to attempt to complete the Meditation to the Water Element. Since you will never leave the comfort of your own home, it will likely be much easier for you to do the Meditation, and you will learn something about yourself in the process. Keep your Life Elements Journal handy so you can write down impressions, messages, and thoughts after you have completed the Meditations.

Chapter 13
Guided Meditations to the Elements

One of the best ways to acquaint yourself with the Elements after you have taken the EDAT is to go visit them. The following are Guided Meditations to each Element. Each Meditation will take you on an imaginary journey. Go through the Meditation that corresponds to your Designated Element(s). If you have Internet connectivity, go to http://www.LifeElements.info. Click the "Meditations" button (the password is "peace" without the quotes) and click the link to the appropriate Guided Meditation. The first of these Meditations is to the Earth Element; the others follow.

If it is easy for you to read the Meditation and put yourself into the story of it, please feel free to do so. However, I have always felt that Guided Meditations are best completed when there is someone actually guiding us. It is then easier fully to immerse ourselves in the story world of the Meditation, and we can then relax and release ourselves to reap the full benefit of the experience. Thus, I have also made these Meditations available online. Find a time when you will not be disturbed and then go to the website, and you will be able to go through the Meditations while fully releasing and relaxing into them.

Give yourself sufficient time to complete the Meditation and allow yourself to step into the world of the story. Then, write up your reactions and feelings to it in your Life Elements Journal.

Guided Meditation to the Earth Element

Note: If you have Internet connectivity, go to http://www. LifeElements.info. Click the "Meditations" button (the password is "peace" without the quotes) and click the link "Guided Meditation to the Earth Element."

This Meditation will take you to the Element of Earth. Earth is our planet. Earth is our home, and as such, Earth is the keeper of our stability. The Element of Earth is difficult to separate from the Earth itself. The deep, rich soil, the forests, the mountains, the stones, the bedrock, and even the molten center of the planet all contribute to our stability. So, when we think about conducting a Meditation to the Element of Earth, we are really thinking about going to any place in or on the land surface of the Earth. The Earth provides solid, stable ground for us to walk upon. The Earth provides nourishment and sustenance in the form of grown food. The Earth provides plants to eat and to use, and the building materials that build our homes. In short, the Earth gives us stability and comfort both on the meditative plane and on the real, physical, tangible plane of our existence.

There are many places to visit so we can encompass and appreciate the vast stability of the Earth. It is because of these many, interconnected aspects of the Earth Element that we can find peace and grounding when communing with it. These aspects form a web of support. If we can trust the Earth will support us, then we can relax and allow ourselves to feel peace and contentment because we feel an inherent sense of abundance and stability.

Lie down comfortably on your bed or on a couch. If you need to put pillows or cushions on or around you to help you feel comfortable, please do so. As you lie down, I want you to allow your toes and feet to relax. Let them gently settle into the place where you are lying. Acknowledge they are solid and real, and imagine they form a connection to the place on which they lie.

Now, imagine that your calves form a gentle connection to what surrounds them. They are part of it, and are therefore softly anchored to it.

Now, allow the same thing to happen to your knees and thighs. Feel how your pelvis, your genitals, and your hips also become more connected as they relax. Allow your belly and your organs also to release. Even as you feel your lungs breathing and your body filling and emptying of breath, let it all connect down. Let your arms, shoulders, neck, and head all loosen as you lie there. Now, soften your eyes, relax your tongue in your mouth, and slowly slacken and relax your jaw.

In this relaxed state, allow the sounds around you to fade into the background. Let the sound of my voice lead you as you let the place you are lying fall away. As you float, gently bring into your mind's eye that you are on a picnic blanket. See yourself on a green-and-white checkered blanket on which you lie comfortably. You have just finished a picnic of delicious sandwiches, and you feel satiated.

The grass and soil below the blanket provide a soft and secure bed for you. As you lie on this blanket with your entire body relaxed, you can sense the sun shining down on you. It feels warm and soothing, and it begins to lull you into an even more relaxed and lazy state. You know if you were to open your eyes right now, you would see a bright sky. In your mind's eye, see the blue of the afternoon sky and the white clouds that lazily make their way across it. Look over and see a stand of green and growing trees nearby. They are tall, sturdy oaks that have lived a long time. Their branches stretch skyward, and their leaves are full of the summer's heat. The soil and grass below you are also full of the summer's heat, and you lie and revel in the tranquil, easy day.

As you enjoy the day, you begin to feel warmth spread through you, and you gently move your hands on either side of the blanket until you can feel the grass on which you lie. The grass feels warm to the touch, and yet you find yourself wanting to feel a bit of the moist soil underneath the grass. So you gently spread the blades of grass until you can see the rich, dark soil below. Slowly, you let a finger brush against the soil. It feels smooth, yet a bit gritty as you touch it. Now, your other fingers and then your entire hand are lightly touching the moist soil. You feel both the roots of the blades of grass and the rich fertile soil.

Now, take a bit of soil in your hand and look closely at it. Honor this bit of soil, for it represents the soil that grows our food and provides us with so much. As you hold the soil in your hand, gently lower your hand to the ground and place the soil back on the surface. As you do so, allow a memory to come back to you. Whether or not it is your own memory, remember it as if it was yours. Remember when you were a young child, and you played in the local playground sandbox. You made patties and forts out of the sand in which you played. For a moment, you simply revel in remembering how you played with mud pies when you were a child. They could be bricks or hamburgers, and they provided endless hours of amusement and fun. Remember how the soil felt as you made patties out of it, and the simple joy of being safe to roam and play.

Remember yourself in dirty clothes, running around and laughing joyfully. Recall one time when a friend had gotten hold of a shovel, and you and he decided to dig for buried treasure in the backyard. You now find yourself in that backyard. Choose a spot where you will begin your hunt near a tall oak tree. Take a look at the tree before you begin to dig. Notice its base and the roots that dig into the ground at the surface.

Now, bring your attention back to the ground, and to the spot where you have chosen to dig. What does it look like here? Is there grass? Is the grass long or short? See the colors of the blades of grass before you touch them. Run your hand along the grass and gently, slowly, remove the grass, and then begin to dig into the rich soil in earnest. Let your young, strong body remove shovelful after shovelful of soil until you have a hole big enough to climb into and explore.

Feeling safe and gleeful, climb into the hole to look around. The first thing you notice is that the soil is different colors as you look lower and lower. What colors do you see? If you reach out to touch it, how does it feel? Is it moist and cool, or dry? It is simply soothing from the heat of the day. You also notice it feels good and safe to sit in the hole with the soil.

Now as you look around, you notice that the roots of the tall oak tree extend to one edge of your hole. You can see how they are wrapped around and hold fast to the soil. The roots seem to provide an anchor to hold the tall tree in place. Even when the tree sways in the wind it never falls over, because its roots are entwined in the soil to give the tree purchase. There have been times, during storms, when you have seen this tree be rocked to and fro, but its roots have held it steady. Now as you look at how the roots are entwined in the soil, you can see how the earth provides a stable home for the roots, so the roots can provide a stable foundation for the tree.

As you sit in the hole, put your feet solidly on the bottom. Let your feet really make the connection to the soil, and almost dig into it as you ground yourself to it. Now, imagine you have roots like the tree. The roots sprout gently from the bottoms of your feet and touch the soil. Imagine the feeling of your "feet roots" penetrating the soil. Let those roots slowly inch their way down, through the bottom of the hole and into the soil there. The soil feels soft yet stable as your feet roots burrow into it. It gives so you can move through, but even as it yields, you can tell as you go deeper it will provide strength for you when you sway.

As you grow more into the soil, remember to look at the hole you have dug. See the soil and notice its foundation. It is here, from the soil's ability to carefully hold the roots entrusted to it, that you can get your own stability. Now that your own roots have burrowed into the soil, you are held gently but securely in its stable embrace. Take some time here and simply enjoy the feeling of being held secure and stable, of being rooted by your connection to the Earth.

After time spent being held gently rooted to the earth, you realize you have grown hot and tired, and you feel like lying down. You slowly begin to lift your feet from the bottom of the hole, and you know even as you do this that your roots are still holding fast in the soil, and it will keep you secure and stable as you walk upon the earth. Now, climb out of the hole and look at the big tree that sits in the Earth just as securely as you do. You have that same stability, the same roots as this oak. You are as solidly anchored to the earth. Keep this in your mind as you move forward.

Walk over a bit and lie down on the soft grass. Put your hands out and feel its texture and warmth. Feel the sense of stability that comes from relaxing and releasing to the gentle pull of the earth. Allow your fingers to play with the blades and as you do so, the memory of that day of treasure hunting begins to fade from your mind. You find yourself back on the sunny day of your picnic. You are still playing with the blades of grass at your sides. You are lying on the green-and-white checkered picnic cloth and the sun touches your skin with its warmth. You feel relaxed and peaceful and sated from your picnic. And as you lie comfortably on your blanket, allow that peaceful state to soothe you even farther into the earth. You feel warm and safe, and you close your eyes to enjoy this lovely day.

Now allow the light of the sun to fade. Whereas it has been a lovely light on your face, allow that light to change into the light that exists in the space where you have been lying here and now. Note the quality of the light you see behind your closed lids. Slowly begin to bring yourself back. Bring your awareness back to your body. As you had been playing with the blades of grass, gently wiggle your fingers now. As you had walked on the soil, gently move your feet now. Retain that sense of peace and stability that came from being in the soil. Keep the sense of safety from being protected by the large tree, and yet you are now back in the present moment. Slowly, gently, move your limbs, and sway them like the branches of that tree. Let them move you into the present as you release the memory and open your eyes.

This Meditation allows you to bring into focus the peace and stability that comes from being rooted in the Earth Element. You have now taken a big first step in developing and maintaining that connection. The next time you feel buffeted by winds, bring yourself back to the safe and rooted feeling you felt while your feet dug roots into the soil. This feeling of stability will come back to you when it is needed. In time, you will find you can truly rely on it being present in any situation.

Eventually, it will be as if you have another method by which to receive events in your life. Whereas often we find ourselves reacting to events before we have fully received and processed them, the presence of the Earth Element allows us to be rooted and receptive to what life has to offer. Then, when we are stable and secure, we can act from this centered place. The decisions we make and the actions we take, and how we feel about those actions, will come from a more unwavering place than we might believe possible.

It will likely take some time for this feeling of stability to become second nature. Yet, you will indeed find yourself rooted, stable, and centered in the earth, and this will change how you act in the world on a permanent and beneficial level.

How do you proceed?

- If you are honoring the Earth Element before continuing on to mitigate an Earth Imbalance, please go back to the Fire Element Missions and Meditations on page 199 to continue.
- If you are honoring the Earth Element before continuing on to integrate other Elements, go to page 173 to keep working on Element Integration.
- If you are at the point in the process where you are integrating the Earth Element into your Element pool, please continue to page 185.

Guided Meditation to the Air Element

Note: If you have Internet connectivity, go to http://www. LifeElements.info. Click the "Meditations" button (the password is "peace" without the quotes) and click the link "Guided Meditation to the Air Element."

Find a comfortable space to sit or lie down. If you plan to be indoors, please choose a spot that will allow you to see out of a window. The first time you do the following Meditation, try it during the day, on a day where the weather is sunny and when there are few clouds in the sky. If you are outdoors, find a spot where you will not be disturbed for the fifteen or so minutes it will take to complete this Meditation.

Lie comfortably. Make sure you have plenty of cushioning around you, so your body is able to relax fully before you begin the Meditation.

Close your eyes and take five deep breaths. Let them be deep, but easy. When you inhale, concentrate on filling your lungs from the bottom up. Feel the air moving into your lungs, and then into the rest of your body. Imagine the air cleansing you and giving you peaceful energy.

Now, open your eyes and look out of the window. Notice the color of the sky. Describe the color to yourself in words that make sense to you. Is it a bright blue? Or is it perhaps lighter and more of a baby blue? Notice if the color of the sky changes as you look toward the horizon. Does it become lighter?

Turn your eyes to look as high up as you can, and acknowledge and describe to yourself the color you see as you look into the sky. Look at any clouds that appear in your line of sight. Are there specific shapes? Are they up high in the sky, or are they down low? Are they shaped like mounds of popcorn, or more like long, folded layers or blankets? Or are the clouds wispy, like a horse's mane? There might, of course, be combinations of clouds in the sky. Notice their color and shape, and most especially acknowledge their difference from the sky around them.

Now, turn your attention back to the sky. Notice how far you can see. We tend to take for granted that we are actually seeing for miles when we look up into the sky. Most particularly if the day outside is clear, we can see clearly for a long distance. Despite the fact that the atmosphere curves around us, we can still use our eyes to locate and identify objects vast distances away.

As you look into the far reaches of the sky, allow your eyelids to become heavy. As your eyelids begin to drift closed, let the sky be the last thing you see. Let the image of the colors, the distance, and the clarity remain in your mind as you continue to breathe deeply and fully. Keep the sky image in your mind's eye as you relax even more. Relax your legs and feet, and let them flow more fully into where they lie. Allow your arms and hands to rest gently, and uncurl your fingers so they are relaxed as well. Let your torso release down into where you lie. And now allow your neck and head to relax against the cushions. Let them both release as you settle yourself even deeper into a state of relaxation. Take a deep breath.

Remember the sky as it was when you had gazed on it. See the sky behind your closed lids and keep it in your mind. Slowly, as you lie here, let that memory wash over you. Allow it to trickle slowly down your body, until you feel yourself take on some of those characteristics. If you were to let them, your arms and legs might easily float up as if they are made of clouds.

The clarity of the sky and the feeling of weightlessness of the clouds are all part of who you are now. And since they are part of you, and since you are part of them, allow your body to begin to feel as light as the clouds you saw. Notice that you might feel as if you can float. Gently imagine allowing yourself to float slightly up from the pillows that cushion you.

As your mind's eye sees and gazes on that sky, notice that you yourself are becoming like the sky and the clouds: weightless, transparent, and yet a part of all that is around you. Allow yourself to experience fully what it means to be pure air. You can float along like a cloud, or you can be simply present in the truth of being the tiny particles that make up the air we all breathe. As you reach and get the sense of floating in your mind's eye, imagine your body rising gently, until you are floating above where you had been lying. Now, with this imagined body, open the window and float out to the air. Feel the breeze on your skin as you gently glide up on the softness of your breath alone. Look at the earth below you, and then look at the clouds floating around you as you rise up to meet them. If you look at yourself, at your hands, allow them to be as blue as the sky, so they are almost translucent and look like clouds or sky to you.

You are the far-seeing truth and clarity that is sky and clouds. You float among them and are part of them, as if you are a bird flying on the thermals. Feel yourself move along the winds and breezes, and know you are perfectly safe because you are a part of this air and sky. You belong here, among the clouds.

Let the gentle breeze lift you up. Glide up above the trees and buildings. Notice how the earth below you becomes smaller as you rise. Take a moment here. From this vantage point, see all that is around you. With this perspective, this bird's eye view, you can see things as they really are, for you see the whole of them.

Now float up, toward the deep blue of the sky, until you are flying among the clouds. Reach out and touch them. Feel their billowy softness as your hand passes through them. From the surface of the earth, the clouds seem to have substance, but here, among them, you can see they are nothing more than vapor. Here, among them, you can see for yourself the truth of what they are.

Look down and really let yourself feel how much you belong up here, where you can see the truth of everything. Here, you can see the big picture with perfect clarity. Allow yourself to float in a full circle, so you can take in everything. Let your mind open to all the possibilities of thought. Allow it to expand so your awareness grows larger and more encompassing. Each new thing you learn and each new truth simply adds to your knowledge of all there is. Your intelligence shines through in this state, for you are part of the Element of Air: the Element of truth, thought, intelligence, reason, and the mind. Like the great eagle or hawk, you can soar to limitless places in your mind.

Stay in this place of learning and thinking. Float among the truth and clarity of sight, of cloud, and of sky. Learn what the Element of Air can teach you. Seek from the Air its basic secret of seeing the truth and being able to think things through because you have enough perspective and clarity to do so. Take it in and make it part of yourself. Float here for now, and be with Air.

You have communed with the Element of Air, and you have been shown new ways of thinking and new ways of using your mind. You have seen a new way to gain a fuller perspective by using the bird's-eye view of the Air Element. Do not be surprised if your way of thinking about things changes from now on. You will more easily seek and find the truth, for the clarity of Air is now within your reach whenever you have need of it.

Having learned some of the basic secrets of seeing the truth of the matter, thank the Air Element, and then begin to take your leave of the sky. Look around once more and say farewell to the sky and the clouds. Now, look down toward the earth, and still knowing you are safe, begin to think once again about your breath. Allow your breath to begin to guide you back down toward the earth at an easy, leisurely pace. There is something exhilarating, yet peaceful about your journey. Know you can come back up to the Air at any time, and that you have learned much.

As you make your way back to where you began, allow your body to welcome your spirit back into itself. Lie back against the cushions and feel yourself settle back into your physical body. Allow yourself to see what is behind your closed lids. Feel your fingers and toes, and allow them some movement by wiggling them gently. Very gently, point and flex your toes. Now, make loose fists with your fingers, and then release them. Softly rotate your wrists and ankles. You will find you feel relaxed and peaceful after your journey. Take three deep breaths. Inhale. Exhale. Inhale. Exhale. Inhale. Exhale.

When you are ready, open your eyes and find yourself back in your original space. Things might look different to you now, because you will see with different eyes.

Take your Life Elements Journal and write down any thoughts or ideas you had during this Guided Meditation. You can do this Meditation at any time you feel the need to connect with the perspective and clarity of the Air Element and with your thoughts, ideas, reason, and truth.

My note to you: If you want to use this same Meditation to find clarity on one of your life issues, do the same Meditation, but allow that issue to be what you view when you begin to glide up to the sky. Let it spread out before you like a panoramic view, and as you rise into the air, you will see the whole of it. This will give you clarity and truth, and you might find yourself gaining insight into the issue as you see it from that bird's-eye view.

How do you proceed?

- If you are honoring the Air Element before continuing on to mitigate an Air Imbalance, please go back to the Water Element Missions and Meditations on page 211 to continue.
- If you are honoring the Air Element before continuing on to integrate other Elements, go to page 199 to keep working on Element Integration.
- If you are at the point in the process where you are integrating the Air Element into your Element pool, please continue to page 173.

Guided Meditation to the Fire Element

Note: If you have Internet connectivity, go to http://www. LifeElements.info. Click the "Meditations" button (the password is "peace" without the quotes) and click the link "Guided Meditation to the Fire Element."

This Meditation will take you to the Element of Fire. Fire is the force of passion, action and creation. It is both destructive and creative. Fire rarely leaves unchanged whatever it touches. Somehow, things will be different. For this Meditation, you will need to light a candle about five feet in front of where you will sit. Please make sure the candle is in a safe place, and will not topple as it burns.

Sit relaxed in a chair. Put a cushion at your back to help you ease into a comfortable sitting position. Do not choose a chair into which you will sink, because for this Meditation, you need to sit in a chair that will allow you to be relaxed but prepared to move.

Once you have the pillow set up and you are comfortable, relax against the back of the chair. Feel your spine as it curves along the pillow and the chair back. Notice how your hips have made themselves comfortable along the seat. Take note of your legs, your thighs and calves, and feel their strength. Honor the work they do to get you from and to every place you need to go.

Now, move your awareness down to your feet and honor their tireless work as well. Your body is always in some form of motion. It is the action and passion of the Fire Element that encourage you to move.

Now spend some time honoring your torso and arms, as well as your shoulders and head. In fact, take a moment and rub your hands along your arms to feel the muscles under the skin. Regardless of what kind of shape we are in, our arms and hands do much for us, and it is best to honor that which they create.

Now, as you bring your awareness to your face, slowly allow your mouth to open in a wide grin. Remember the last time you genuinely smiled, and honor that moment of joy. Bring your awareness to your eyes. As you become more aware of your eyes, bring your gaze to the candle. Slowly, look at the candle's flame from the top to the bottom. Notice if it is moving and flickering. Pay close attention to what it looks like, and when you are ready, let the candle flame be the last thing you see as you close your eyes. Breathe deeply, and imagine you are inhaling the rich, sweet scent of wood smoke.

The chair on which you are sitting is now a richly decorated throne. It is made of the softest reeds, and it is comfortable and familiar. There are richly woven fabrics in yellows and reds at your feet, and the scent of tropical night-blooming flowers fills the air. In this place, you look around and see your people, who have gathered for this great rite and holiday. Meet their eyes and acknowledge them warmly, for they are here to support you on your quest. Take in the blankets and food that have been collected in the clearing and inhale the intoxicating scents of the night.

Finally, bring your eyes to the center of the clearing. Here you see your true purpose. The young men of the tribe have already begun building the tinder of the grand bonfire. Tonight, your son has the honor of lighting the fire into which you will go.

You are a Kahuna, an elder of the native peoples of Hawaii. You come from a glorious and proud people who have a long history of performing the ancient, mystical rite of fire walking. You are a firewalker of the old ways. Generations of your family have walked into the midsummer night bonfire, and have moved through it to be changed, but unscathed. Tonight, under the full moon, you will walk the fire.

As you sit on your throne, bring your full attention to the fire pit. Your son says a prayer of the old ways as he gazes on you, and then lays the torch to the tinder. The bonfire roars to life. It is housed in the fire pit, but you recognize it is only barely held there, for even a stray bit of breeze could bring the fire spilling up and over the stones that line the pit. Just like you, a powerful and passionate shaman, Fire is only contained at its own whim, and you recognize and acknowledge your kinship with this transformative force.

As you look around, you see the night is young. The sun has just set, and you begin to see the first stars of the night. While others make their own preparations, you prepare yourself for your rite. You close your eyes and see the dance of light behind your closed lids. Reach out with your mind and touch the life and vitality of the fire. It sinuously moves and ignites what it touches. Each log or sapling that meets the fire is changed by it. It is transformed from one state of being to another. It returns to its most basic form: carbon, the stuff of life.

And now, the drums begin. You hear them being played by the young men of the tribe. Look into the fire and see what it teaches you. Lift yourself from your throne as you are drawn to it. Follow the rhythm of the drums and begin to move toward the fire. Feel its heat begin to warm you as you approach. Listen to the wavering boom of the waves of flame as you approach.

As the fire's strength washes over you, breathe deeply and let it enter your spirit. It changes everything it touches, and it now touches you. Slowly, gently, put your hand into the flames. Feel the heat move over you and through you, but while it changes and consumes the logs it burns, for you, it begins an internal change. You are changed but remain the same as the flames dance over your hand, for you are one with the fire. You breathe gently as you move even closer.

Now, step over the stones and let your foot find purchase in the flames. You feel the heat and a sensation of sizzling, but it is of a spiritual nature as the energy that surrounds you crackles and sizzles over your spiritual body. However, your physical body flows into and with the fire, and remains unhurt. This cleansing for your spirit self does not injure you.

You realize you are like a log as the fire burns it. The log does not simply disappear as it burns. Rather, it is transformed into its new form. It becomes pure energy. Its old state is changed into something brand-new. As you walk among the coals, you feel the flames, but they do not hurt. They are simply molding you into something new as well.

Around you, you see the people dancing joyfully around the fire. Both women and men spin and twirl around the bonfire to give you energy and encouragement. Through the flames, you see their muscles straining as they leap and whirl. You see their hair fly and their limbs in motion as they dance to the beat of the drums. The drums also help you keep your concentration for the task at hand. They and you trade energy as the drummers provide the rhythm for your transformation.

Feel yourself being one with the flames. Feel how the heat melts you and changes you, but your physical body stays the same. And now, the drumbeat changes. It accelerates and grows louder, deeper, more passionate as you prepare for the final achievement. You will leave the fire as you entered it. Your actions will show to all that you are the true firewalker. You are the one who changes as you are changed.

Your belief is strong and your certainty is fierce, and these protect you as you take one last breath inside the flames, gather your strength and will, and then leap gracefully out of the flames and into the night. The music reaches its peak and then overflows and calms as you are greeted by shouts and cries of friends and loved ones. You have completed a glorious task. The fire has been walked, and the village has been blessed for another year.

Slowly, you are led back to your throne, and cool water is brought before you. As you drink deeply, you close your eyes and relax against the great chair. Slowly, your body loosens and you become sleepy. Allow yourself to relax deeply after your great achievement. You have walked the fire in your spirit body. It is now time to rejoin your physical body. Begin to move slowly in your physical body. Let your feet and hands curl and straighten as you begin the motions of this world. Now become aware of the sounds around you. Feel your legs and arms and move them. Allow yourself to return to the here and now.

Feeling relaxed and peaceful, joyful and energetic, breathe deeply as you open your eyes. Your spirit has been transformed. You have walked the fire, and things will never be the same.

How do you proceed?

- If you are honoring the Fire Element before continuing on to mitigate a Fire Imbalance, please go back to the Earth Element Missions and Meditations on page 185 to continue.
- If you are honoring the Fire Element before continuing on to integrate other Elements, go to page 173 to keep working on Element Integration.
- If you are at the point in the process where you are integrating the Fire Element into your Element pool, please continue to page 199.

Guided Meditation to the Water Element

Note: If you have Internet connectivity, go to http://www. LifeElements.info. Click the "Meditations" button (the password is "peace" without the quotes) and click the link "Guided Meditation to the Water Element."

This Meditation will take you to the Element of Water. Water is the center of emotions. When you visit and commune with Water, please be prepared that you will likely experience strong emotions of one sort or another. That is a perfectly normal reaction, and if you do have it, please remember you are absolutely entitled to your emotions, and you can accept them as a part of you as you feel them.

Lie down comfortably on your bed. If you need to put pillows or cushions on or around you to help you feel comfortable, please do so. Begin to breathe slowly and deeply as you find just the right position in which to lie. Make yourself as comfortable as possible.

Now, I want you to allow your toes and feet to relax. Let them gently flow into the place where you are lying and release downward. Imagine they are no longer quite so solid, and they melt into the bed. Now, imagine your calves slowly melting and flowing outward, as if they are liquid. Allow the same thing to happen to your knees and thighs. Feel your pelvis, your genitals, and your hips also become more malleable as they relax down onto the bed. Your belly and your organs also relax.

Take a moment here to note how fluid most of your body actually is. We are made mostly of water, and this consciousness of your own fluidity is what you begin to access as you feel yourself melt gently into the bed. Even as you feel your lungs breathing and your body filling and emptying of breath, let it all simply float down. Let your arms, shoulders, neck, and head all relax as you float downward.

Behind your closed eyelids, acknowledge whatever it is you see in your mind's eye. Whatever thoughts are flowing into your awareness, allow them to flow through you, as if they are simply water dropping through the air.

Now, bring your awareness to your thoughts in such a way that you almost see them before you release them. Allow them to slow, as if you are falling asleep even while you remain awake and aware. As they slow, gently begin to guide your thoughts with your mind. Lightly nudge your thoughts to the last time you were at the beach. Was the beach on a lake, or was it on an ocean? Whichever one it was, find one memory from a time at the beach when you were near the water. Do you remember what the water looked like as you sat on the sand? Did you swim? If so, do you remember what the water felt like? Cast yourself back to that moment. Remind yourself of the feeling, sight, and sound of the waves coming onto shore.

Now, place yourself on a blanket at that beach, and wherever it was, allow it to become a beach on the ocean. The sand beneath you is white and warm from the sun. There are seagulls flying overhead, playing on the breeze. You watch the waves as they roll and play with the shore. Slowly, you get up off your blanket and make your way across the hot sand, until you reach the water's edge. Here the sand is cooler, and wet as your feet lightly sink into it. Your feet are getting wet, and a wave gently comes in and gets you wet up to your ankles. What does this moment in time feel like to you? Do you have a reaction unlike what you might have expected? What do you feel about this moment? Do you feel exhilarated? Happy? Or do you find yourself a bit nervous to be near so much water? Even if you are nervous about it, you find yourself fascinated by the play of light, sand, and water.

Now, walk slowly, deeper into the waves. You feel perfectly at home here at the water's edge. The waves feel cool against your warm skin, but they are not threatening. They are simply moving along as they are carried by the tides and by the moon. As you stand and allow yourself to be a part of the motion of the water, you find yourself feeling as if you are a part of that connection between the ocean and the moon. Somehow, you have tapped into the ocean's secret. It simply moves as it is moved. Its tides are reactions to the pull from the moon, from the landmasses the ocean surrounds, and from the bottom depths from which so much comes.

Now, turn and walk deeper into the ocean, and as you do, continue to feel perfectly at home. It is as if you have lived here all your life.

In fact, in your imagination, allow yourself to believe you are one of the mythical mermaids or mermen who lived in the depths of the seas. You feel so comfortable, it is almost as if instead of legs, you have a tail to support and propel you. You feel safe as you reach a depth where you can no longer stand and you gently lower your entire body into the water. You realize you have been swimming comfortably for some time now. You also find you can breathe quite comfortably under the water's surface.

Open your eyes underwater and take in what is laid out before you. Are there beautiful sea anemones? Are there fish? Dolphins? Whales? Gaze upon the beauty of these depths. Allow yourself to feel the wonder of seeing and being a part of this incredible world.

As you swim along, you will notice a dolphin has swum up rather close to you. Neither of you feels afraid of the other, and yet, some emotions do well up inside you. Take a moment here as you gaze upon this denizen of the deep. Notice what the dolphin looks like. Look at her shape; see her fins and flippers. Look closely at her face and eyes. See for yourself what she has to show you as you look at her. Now, take a moment and acknowledge exactly what you are feeling right now. Are you happy? Are you nervous? Do you feel joy at connecting with this being, or is there some apprehension around being here right now? What do you feel?

Remember that if you feel at all apprehensive, you are perfectly safe in this place and time. The dolphin is here to serve as guide and protector for you. You are here because you wish to be, and can leave at any time. Knowing this makes it easier to stay and explore the seascape. Allow yourself to explore this watery environment. Note and remember what you see and what you feel as you come across new things and beings.

These reactions you are having are the heart of feelings. Being suspended in water is like being in the womb, where we were safe and all of our needs were met through the fluids that nourished and sustained us. The ocean of the womb is where we come from, and it is where the secret to our hearts truly lies.

Swim into the darker depths, and realize you can see clearly. Acknowledge what you see, touch, and hear, and most importantly, what you feel as you dive even deeper into your emotional center.

Down here, in the deep, the ocean's tides are not felt as strongly. Here it is calmer, for it is close to the center. As you float here, you come to the realization that although there is still life and motion in the deepest part, it is also somehow more still because of its very depth, its proximity to your center. Just like the ocean, the strong and sometimes volatile emotions of our surface selves can have a real stillness in their depths. We can find a sense of calm below the surface. As you float, you realize your surface emotions are often reactions to external stimuli. You have feelings about what others have said or done. However, you can also clearly see that your calm center does not move, regardless of what occurs on the surface. A storm that creates the waves above might never reach the depths of stillness below.

When you feel fear, when you feel jealousy, when you feel anger, it is as a response to external stimuli. Yet, when you feel the deeper emotions, they are the ones that come from inside you. Just as the ocean depths are calm and still because they are not responding to external surface stimuli, your innermost emotions can be calm and still as well.

Here at these depths of the ocean and at these depths of your emotions, you can find your inner space of peace and wonder, just as you wondered at the joyful dolphins. You stand at the crossroads of these depths, for you are the intermediary between them.

Spend a moment, here at the depths of the ocean, at the deepest part of your core self, and honor your feelings of stillness and calm. Regardless of where your emotions take you in your daily life, you now know that at their core is peace and stillness. You can return to this stillness, this peace, at any time.

As you float in the depths, breathe in and out, gently and slowly. Notice the air bubbles as they begin to rise on your exhalations. Slowly, follow them up and allow yourself to become more aware of the sounds around you in the here and now. As you move toward the surface of the water, allow your consciousness to move toward the surface of your awareness.

Let your awareness of your current surroundings increase as you slowly, gently, begin to move your fingers and toes where you are presently lying. As you leave the ocean depths in your mind, allow yourself to fully reenter the here and now. Feeling refreshed and relaxed, move your body against the fabric of the cushions, pillows, and blankets. When you are fully back to the present, open your eyes. See where you are, and reconnect with what you are currently feeling.

You have taken a marvelous step on the path to your emotional core. Write any of your reactions and feelings in your Life Elements Journal. Spend some time contemplating your feelings, and let them guide you forward.

How do you proceed?

- If you are honoring the Water Element before continuing on to mitigate a Water Imbalance, please go to the Air Element Missions and Meditations on page 173 to continue.
- If you are honoring the Water Element before continuing on to integrate other Elements, go to page 199 to keep working on Element Integration.
- If you are at the point in the process where you are integrating the Water Element into your Element pool, please continue to page 211.

Chapter 14
Introduction to Missions and Meditations

Now we are entering the next phase of the Integration Process. You have assessed your Elemental status, and now it is time to implement the changes that will complete the process. These Missions and Meditations are designed to work with the same basic principles as cognitive behavioral therapy and similar techniques. Put into simple terms, if you do something long enough, it worms its way into your mind and then changes your patterns. The pieces of what we will undertake in the following will coalesce to make lasting changes to your manner of interacting and existing in your world.

With these Missions and Meditations, you will increase your familiarity and comfort with the individual Elements in the appropriate order. One of the most important aspects of these Missions is that you take the time to really delve into each of them. Please note: It might take a while to get through the book in its entirety, because each of these Missions and Meditations can be repeated. Each time, the results will bring you a bit closer to accessing fully the Element you wish to cultivate. It is of vital importance to jump into the Missions with both feet, regardless of whether they feel silly or uncomfortable. In fact, the Missions that initially feel the most uncomfortable might well be the ones on which you most need to focus. It is only by releasing yourself into the intimate experience of the moment that you will reap the full benefits of the Missions and be able to reach your integration goals. Note that the Missions can be helpful even if they feel silly and you do them only halfheartedly. They are designed to help you gain greater knowledge of your most intimate self, and they will help you access your creativity, your peacefulness, and your emotional and passionate nature. I do wish to say, though, they will help you best if you try them with full commitment. You will be extremely surprised at the results.

We have previously covered the necessary steps in the Integration Process. The reason for the process is that as you become more intimately acquainted with each Element, you will find that some of your instinctive responses might begin to change and evolve into something new. Whereas before you began this journey you might have had an instinctual response to certain stimuli, you might find what you first want to do or say changes based on what you internalize from each Element's characteristics. For example, when faced with feelings of loneliness or isolation, some of us turn to a varied and perhaps hectic social life. We might engage in activities not in our best interest. For some reason (and according to this book, it is a Fire Imbalance), we keep repeating those patterns that are possibly even harmful to us. If we are not centered in our self-knowledge, we might find ourselves floundering and seeking both approval and a sense of belonging in patterns of behavior that are too impulsive and perhaps rash. These actions will not give us that sense of belonging, because the crucial piece of feeling centered is missing. That centered feeling is a connection to and kinship with the Earth Element.

The following Missions and Meditations will help you complete the Integration Process. Please note: It might take several completions of the Missions to integrate a particular Element into your patterns (I will create new Missions to supplement this core set. Visit LifeElements.info for information.) This challenge will be most apparent when you attempt to access your primary Element's polar opposite. It is highly likely you will have a difficult time accessing your Designated Element's polar opposite. You are more than up to the challenge of this, and yet I ask you to treat yourself with kindness as you embark on these Missions. They are challenging, and they will make you think. They will change some of your perceptions about yourself and the world around you. You are to be commended for getting to this point and for persevering in your personal quest to find peace and contentment, and to achieve your goals.

Here, a word of care: As you cultivate the Elements, you will doubtless feel tension: a push-pull in various directions. This push-pull will make you uncertain, because you might feel you used to know what would happen because the Elements were aligned a certain way. Now that things are different, it will be uncomfortable, and you might need to tell yourself you know what you are doing and this will be good for you in the long run. You might wish to look at this phase as growing pains. Despite the fact that there is some discomfort, it is all in the service of creating a better and more self-directed life. If you do find things feel too uncertain, then the first thing to do is to go back to the place of your power. Go back and redo the "Inner Voice" Meditation from page 32 (or at http://LifeElements.info online. Click the "Meditations" button. The password is "peace" without the quotes). Spend a bit of time and reconnect with your strength of spirit and determination. Then, once you feel more centered, continue on the path you have set, and it will feel significantly easier to do so from this calm, centered place.

This can also be applied to decisions you make about the direction in which your life is going, on both the micro and macrocosmic levels. In some ways, everything we do and think is done and thought in response to some stimulus or another. From our beginnings as babies and toddlers, to how we were raised, to the messages we received from parents, family, friends, the media, the government, authority figures, and so on, these all created scenarios in which we had to somehow develop an opinion, have some reaction, make a statement, take a stand, or act in some way in response. Our relative strengths in the different Elements inform and form the responses we make. A Fire person will react very differently than will an Air person (and because that person is a Fire person, the reaction will be much more active in nature than the more cerebral reaction of an Air person). However, everyone will have some reaction to everything, whether or it is a reaction done in thought, feeling, acceptance, or motion. Remember, the Elements that are present and influencing the person at the time of the occurrence of the situation dictate what the response will be. The Missions below will give you access to the Elements in such a way that you will be able to choose the most appropriate one with which to proceed.

Chapter 15
Air Missions and Meditations

1. Air Meditation: Get In Touch With Your Deepest Breath

Note: If you have Internet connectivity, go to http://www. LifeElements.info. Click the "Meditations" button (the password is "peace" without the quotes) and click the link "Air Meditation: Get In Touch With Your Deepest Breath."

This Meditation is designed to help you get in touch with your breath. We often forget to breathe deeply, and in fact most of the time, we only breathe with the top one-third of our lungs. This is what is known as shallow breathing. In order to get fully comfortable with our breath and by extension the Air Element, it is vital for us learn to breathe deeply and fully. Yoga as a practice concentrates a good deal on the breath and deep, full inhalations and exhalations.

To complete this Mission, find some time when you will not be disturbed for about fifteen minutes. Sit down comfortably. If possible, sit cross-legged on the floor on a cushion or pillow. If this is too uncomfortable, sit on a cushioned couch or chair and make sure your feet are flat on the floor and your back is straight.

Place the palms of your hands on your knees. Close your eyes and take a deep breath in and out. Do it again, and this time try to notice if your shoulders raised and lowered when you did so. If they did, then I will ask you to try again, and this time relax your abdominal muscles and try to breathe into your belly so that your belly expands when you inhale and contracts when you exhale.

If you find it challenging to breathe into your belly without raising your shoulders, take a moment to complete the following procedure.

Lie down on your back and place a standard-size paperback book on your belly. Take a deep breath. You might notice that as you inhale the book rises, and as you exhale the book lowers. You might also notice that when you are lying down, your shoulders do not rise on inhalation. This is ideal, so please practice it a few more times to get the hang of it. Stay relaxed as you breathe, and you will naturally find your breathing works in this way. Once you have achieved some comfort with this type of breathing, go back to the Meditation and begin again.

Sit with your feet flat on the floor and your spine is straight. Breathe in, and let your stomach expand as you take in the air. Let it contract as you exhale. As you breathe like this, imagine that your torso is an urn about to be filled with water. The water flows in and fills the urn from the bottom up. That is the optimal way for the breath to move into and out of your body. Let your belly expand as you breathe in and then let it contract as you exhale.

Another way to try it is to put one of your hands on your belly. Try to imagine the air going down as deep as your hand as you inhale. When you feel it happening, allow the air to empty out as you exhale. Try this a few more times. Once you have that down, put your other hand on your ribs at the side of your torso. Breathe in, and let the first part of your breath move into your belly. Then, once that part of your body feels full, allow the breath to move into your sides, and feel your sides expand with the breath. The intercostal muscles, which are the muscles between your ribs, expand and contract when you breathe. Allow those muscles to expand at your sides as you take the second part of this full breath. Then, when it is time to exhale, breathe out, first from your sides, and then empty the breath from your belly.

Try this a few more times. Breathe into your hand that rests on your belly. Then continuing the same breath, breathe into your sides. Now, exhale from your sides and then complete the exhalation from your belly.

Try it again twice more. As you breathe, remain in the same position as before with your back straight and your legs relaxed.

After a few more completed breaths, it is time to incorporate the next part of this breathing technique. Once you have inhaled into your belly and into your sides, complete the breath by inhaling into your chest. If your shoulders lift a bit at this point, it is fine, since this is the last step in filling your lungs and your upper torso will naturally expand a bit as your lungs fill fully.

Try this a few times. Inhale into your belly, and then into your sides, and now into your chest. Exhale first from the chest, and then from your sides, and last from your belly.

Try this a few times. Once you have the knack of breathing while staying relaxed, it is time to incorporate the last bit of this breathing technique as follows.

Continuing this same breathing method, now put your hands on your knees very lightly. As you begin to inhale deeply into your belly, and then your sides and upper chest, gently begin to arch your back. Feel your spine curve as you slowly inhale and look up. Do not go farther than it is comfortable to go when you arch your back. When you are full of breath, gently begin your exhalation, and as you exhale, begin to round your back. Let your eyes guide you as you flow from looking up to looking down, and your back gently curves and rounds.

Try this again. Inhale gently as you arch your back, and now exhale as you round your back. Try to make the length of the inhalation match the time it takes you to arch your back fully. Do the same with the exhalation.

Gently inhale and arch your back. Feel your body expand as you breathe in. Feel the air come into your body. Now exhale and round your back fully. Let your hands on your knees be your guide as you gently move to the rhythm of your breath. You find that a gentle sense of peace begins to pervade your entire being. You feel serene and relaxed. Allow your thoughts to flow as you breathe and find them to be restful and relaxing.

Keep the air moving into and out of your body. Gradually, let it become more relaxed, and allow yourself to move back into your normal mode of breathing. Once your breath returns to its natural state, take a minute to assess how you feel now. How are your thoughts moving through your mind? How is your outlook?

Allow yourself to be at peace.

Do this "arched breath" ten times, and see how you feel when you are done. Note any reactions, thoughts, or insights in your Journal. You might notice you feel calm and peaceful. From this state, you can begin to see things without judgment. You can begin to see the truth. This is the beginning of the clarity of Air.

2. Air Mission: Draw the Apple

Turn to a blank page of your Life Elements Journal and grab a pencil of any kind. Allow the pencil's point to rest gently in the center of the piece of paper. Close your eyes. Take a few deep breaths, and then behind your closed eyes, picture an apple. You have seen them dozens and perhaps hundreds of times, and you now see it with your inner eye. Remember the last time you looked at an apple, and perhaps picture that one. Get a really good idea of what the apple looks like in your mind. Is it more round in shape, or more of an oblong shape? Does it have a stem attached to it, and maybe even a leaf?

When you have it in your mind and keeping your eyes closed, let the pencil very gently start sketching the general shape. If it is more of a rounded apple shape, draw a circle and go over that same circle a few times. You do not need to press hard, but you do need to make sure you actually have kind of a circular shape. If your apple is a more oblong shape, go ahead and draw an oval in whichever way your apple is oblong.

You are currently using your imaginative mind to think through and visualize what it is you wish to draw. Then you will do a line-by-line, step-by-step drawing, and create your drawing. This is utilizing your logical, reasoning brain from beginning to end.

Go ahead and keep drawing that circle for another couple more turns, and then once you have finished, while keeping the apple firmly in your mind, remove the pencil from the paper and look at what you have drawn. (Bear in mind that this exercise is judgment-free. Do not worry over the appearance of your drawing. There is no place here to judge yourself harshly on your drawing abilities. This is simply an exercise to access and activate your logical, step-by-step mind. This activity will help bring it awake.)

You will probably see a circle that sort of wanders a bit. That is okay. Just go ahead and keep the apple firmly in your mind, and begin to sketch out something you remember about the apple. Close your eyes and see your apple in your mind's eye. If it is rounded, it still has sort of a little scoop where the stem would normally go. So now, open your eyes and with your pencil, very deliberately draw the scoop where it should appear on your apple. Imagine the location of the scoop on your apple, and then draw it in the exact same spot on the paper. You can go over it a couple of times.

When you are done with the stem, close your eyes and look with your imagination at the bottom of the apple. Does your apple have the little ridges and nubs at the bottom? If so, open your eyes and draw those in as well.

Now, in your mind, remember whether your apple has a stem. If the apple does have a stem, go ahead and draw a stem just how you envision it. Does it curve to the left or to the right? Does it have a leaf attached to it? Draw your leaf as it appears in your mind. If there is no stem, then the apple might be complete, or at least as far as you will go right now.

As you repeat the Missions to keep accessing greater amounts of the Air Element, return to this exercise in the future to fill in more details about your apple as you open and access more and more of your Air mind. You will fill in and flesh out the apple more and more as you get stronger and stronger in Air. The step-by-step process of drawing this apple begins to exercise your thinking muscles.

Remember, do not judge the quality of your drawing as it compares to what you envisioned. Seldom do we draw anything exactly as we envision it. The important thing here is to make the approximation of what you see in your mind, and do it in an orderly, step-by-step fashion.

Now, sign and date your drawing. You will come back to it again. Please note: It is possible to complete this Mission with any number of items. You might wish to visualize other items, and then use the step-by-step thought process of the Air Element to help you draw them out of your imagination and place them on the page. This Mission does an excellent job of cultivating Air by creating that vital connection between the worlds of imagination and tangible reality.

3. Air Mission: Write a Short Story or Poem

This Mission will help spark the thought flow, and the manner in which information filters and is connected in your thinking processes. I will ask you here and now to plan, formulate, and write a short story.

To give you a bit of a hand and get your analytical mind jump-started, I will ask you to write a story that incorporates certain Elements. I will give you a place, a name, a time of year, and an object, and I will ask you to write a story that incorporates all of these words. This means you will have to plan how to make the words all fit into one cohesive story, and then create a reasonable story that incorporates them.

To help you see how it might be done, here is a tale I created of one such exercise. I asked a number of friends to give me various words. I asked for a name, a time of year, a location, and an object. One such set of words was:

Name: Leon

Time of year: February 29th

Location: Subway

Object: Moai statue (the large head statues at Easter Island)

I wrote a story incorporating these four Elements. I used the planning and reasoning aspects of Air to create the characters and plot while incorporating the words above into the story.

First, I thought of the name, Leon. I closed my eyes and thought of what a Leon might be like. To me, he was an older African-American man. In addition, he was down on his luck. The time of year is February 29th and that is a special day, so I decided to see if I could make the day be really special in the story. The location of the subway made my story take place in New York City, and Leon became a homeless man in New York.

The tough part was how to incorporate a Moai statue into the tale. I had to think through various machinations of how a Moai might interact with a homeless man in New York. Finally, I planned it out with an outline and began writing the story. You can find the entire story here: http://www.LifeElements.info/leon.htm.

Here are a few sets of randomly selected groups of words. In your Life Elements Journal, copy one set and plan out a tale that incorporates all four Elements. I will ask that the story be at least 500 words long, to give you some in-depth exposure to the planning and writing process. You might find you wish to make the story longer. If you do, please do so. I would love to see your story, so please feel free to email it to me.

Set 1:
Name: Linda
Time of year: Labor Day weekend
Location: Newport, Rhode Island
Object: Piano

Set 2:
Name: Stanley
Time of year: Christmas Eve
Location: Hospital gift shop
Object: Ice cream cone

Set 3:
Name: Barbara Jo
Time of year: Early spring
Location: Dublin, Ireland
Object: Child's finger paint set

Set 4:
Name: Bobby
Time of year: Late autumn
Location: Hardware store
Object: Crystal vase

Now, let us begin to plan out how you might write the first story. First, open your Life Elements Journal to a blank page, grab a pen or pencil, and write down the words from the first set: *Linda, Labor Day weekend, Newport, Rhode Island*, and *Piano*. Read these words over a few times, and then close your eyes and think about each of the words separately.

What thoughts come to you when you think about Labor Day weekend? Personally, I begin to think of the last weekend of vacation, of getaways, and of barbecues and parties. What are your thoughts about it? Please write them down.

Bring your attention to Newport, Rhode Island. What do you know about it? If you are not familiar with it, then you might want to spend a bit of time doing some research. Certainly, you can plot out a tale without much knowledge of this place, but it might be easier to do a Google search or go to the library and find some information on Newport to flesh it out for yourself. Whatever thoughts and research you do, please write the results in your Life Elements Journal (and remember, thoughts and research are both crucial aspects of the Air Element, so you will reap double the benefits from this portion of the Mission). I will say that Newport used to be a celebrated vacation spot for the wealthy and famous, and its many mansions are still quite splendid. The rest you will want to research and develop yourself.

Now, give some thought to the piano. Is it an old, dilapidated instrument, or is it a grand piano that is beautifully maintained? How might you describe it if someone asked about it? Write your description down in your Life Elements Journal.

Last, let us take a look at the name Linda. When you think of this Linda, is she a young girl or an older woman? Do you get an idea of what she might look like? What might she do for a living? If she finds herself in Newport on Labor Day weekend, is she a socialite, a wealthy older woman with memories, or is she perhaps a maid working at one of the grand mansions? Allow your imagination to roam free, and write down whatever ideas you might have.

With the information written above, begin to look at what things strike you as possibly relating to one another. Are there any direct relationships? If not, then how might you connect them? If Linda is indeed a maid, for example, might she be working to pay for college, and so works Labor Day weekend right up until the end of vacation season? Is she perhaps a music student, and cannot help but sit down at the beautiful Steinway that has been sitting and gathering dust in the drawing room at the Malcolm summer home? This already has the seeds for a moving story of dreams and music. Think of your own ideas from what you have written, and incorporate them into this growing idea. To see my own version of this story, please go to http://LifeElements.info/Missions.htm

Working with this set of words might have already given you an idea of how to begin this tale. If so, please do complete it, and use all four of the concepts/words to write it. Remember to have a beginning, middle, and ending, and you will have a terrific story once you have finished.

If you have not come up with a beginning, I will give you the first sentence: "The sharp trill of the telephone interrupted Linda's thoughts." Write this sentence down and have fun completing Linda's story. Please attempt to write this story by thinking through and writing down all of your ideas. Then, you will want to pick and choose the ones that make sense for you. Follow what you write to its conclusion, and you will be surprised at the lovely tale you tell.

Once you have finished the first one, please write stories for the next three as well. If you need to, research the locations and the objects to fill out your writing. If this means you must buy a child's finger paint set, then have fun and paint!

As you complete this Mission, the stories will become easier and yet more exciting to write. They will challenge you and help you hone the thoughtful deliberation that is such a key part of Air characteristics.

Write each of your stories in your Journal. If you wish to do so, please send them to me at http://LifeElements.info. I would love to read them, and with your permission, to post them on the site to inspire others to follow your example.

This Mission will give you new ways of communicating and thinking. It will hone your writing skills and your analytical mind. You will use these skills in many areas of your life as you become increasingly at home with Air.

4. Air Mission: Cloud Watching

One of the best and simplest ways to honor the Air Element and simultaneously engage your mind and your imagination (the provinces of Air) is to take the time to lie down, quiet your inner tour guide, and cloud watch.

Choose a day that is bright and sunny, and warm enough for you to spend time outdoors. A Saturday afternoon where you are not required to be anywhere for an hour would be perfect. Specifically choose a day that will allow you to spend some time being quiet and relaxed. One of the key aspects of this process is the importance of releasing some of the ingrained thought patterns by consciously relaxing your thinking brain. This really means you can try to acknowledge your many deadlines and the amount of thinking and planning necessary to accomplish your goals, and then you will want to lay them aside for the hour or so you will need for this activity.

Gather a blanket and perhaps some water, and then go out to a place where you will have a clear view of the sky. If you live in an urban area, you might wish to find some place where you will be able and allowed to go up on a roof of a building. Please observe any safety precautions as you do this activity.

Ideally, you will want to do this on a day where there are a lot of cumulus clouds (the big, puffy ones that look like cauliflower or mounds of cotton) in the sky. These make for the best viewing, since they can give you many shapes to see and study.

Please note: As you prepare your viewing space, make sure you orient your blanket in such a way that you will not be looking directly into the sun.

Once you have chosen your viewing spot and laid out your blanket, lie down and close your eyes. Take a few deep breaths. Feel the air move in and out of your lungs. Feel your torso, and even your entire body expanding as you inhale slowly and deeply, and then feel your body contract as you release the air out of your lungs. Let this become a peaceful internal movement as you quietly calm your mind. Allow your thoughts to dissipate slowly.

When a thought enters your mind, take the time to acknowledge it and assure yourself of the certainty that you will deal with the thought eventually, and then release the thought to float along the stream of your mind. Keep doing this until your mind feels at rest. For this time, allow your mind to calm as you lie on your blanket and breathe deeply and steadily.

Once your mind is quiet, slowly open your eyes.

Take notice of the first cloud you see. Allow it to suffuse

your vision. Let your mind produce a picture of what the cloud represents. Do you see the outlines of an object or an animal of some kind? What does the shape conjure up for you? You might feel a spark as the picture of it forms in your mind. Use your imagination to flesh out the shape until the cloud truly represents the image you pictured.

Once you have the image firmly in your mind, acknowledge what you see and how you were able to turn the cloud into your object. Believe it or not, it takes a special skill to see an indistinct shape and symbolically turn it into the image of a dragon or a rabbit.

Now, release your image and look at another cloud. Allow that cloud to give you a mental picture of what it represents. Keep using your imagination and your mind to flesh out the clouds and the images they give you. At some point, you might even wish to write mini-stories of what you saw in the clouds. For now, keep your mind focused solely on what you see, and let it all flow to you and then through you as you honor your mind and its wonderful capabilities of identification, categorization, and imagination.

All this time you have spent watching clouds has been a chance for you to focus and use your mind in a way that might be slightly different from what feels comfortable. This Mission gives you an opportunity to let your mind soar free in your imagination. You can now see and analyze. You can now imagine and transform what you see. This is your special gift.

Once you have spent some time cloud watching, allow your breath to deepen once again. Close your eyes and allow your thoughts to slow as you did before. Acknowledge them as they come into your mind, and then release them so that, soon, you are at peace and gently floating in the serenity and quiet of your mind. When you feel ready, say the words "I honor the Air Element as I honor myself. I honor my thoughts, my intelligence, and my reason, and the truth and clarity that come from Air."

Once again, open your eyes, feeling recharged and refreshed from your sky adventure.

Chapter 16
Earth Missions and Meditations

1. Earth Meditation: Grounding

Note: If you have Internet connectivity, go to http://www. LifeElements.info. Click the "Meditations" button (the password is "peace" without the quotes) and click the link "Earth Meditation: Grounding."

With this Meditation, we will be connecting to the earth below us. We will forge a bond to the solid bedrock of the Earth.

Lie down comfortably on your bed. Place a pillow under your knees to deepen your sense of comfort. Make sure you have low lighting in the room. Perhaps you might want to light a candle or two, so the soft lighting will add to the relaxing atmosphere you want to create for this Meditation.

As you lie down, begin to deepen your breathing. Let it come into your lungs as gently as possible. Allow your breath to leave your body simply and soothingly.

Begin to notice your body. Bring your attention to your toes. Notice how they feel. If you are wearing shoes or socks, try to note how your toes feel in them. If you are barefoot, see if you can feel the air on your toes. Bring your focus to the balls of your feet. Notice the sole and the heel of each foot. Draw your attention to the top of your feet and then your ankles. Notice the bones and the muscles, and take a moment to honor them for them for the work they do to move you through the world.

Now that you have paid attention to your feet, consciously allow them to relax, and let your awareness travel up to your calves. Notice how they lie on the pillow. Draw your attention to your knees.

Notice if they are bent, and how they feel from both the bottom and the top of your legs. If they are at all uncomfortable, shift around until you feel even more relaxed.

Bring your attention to your thighs, both the top and the bottom. See if you can feel them from the outside by feeling your clothes on your skin or the air in the room. Become aware of the large bones and muscles from the inside, be conscious of them as part of your body. Now that you are aware of your legs, relax them and let your awareness of them deepen your relaxed state.

Now bring your attention to your hips, your pelvis, your genitals, and your buttocks. Allow them to relax and release. Bring your attention to your belly, and see if you can sense your organs, your intestines, and the muscles of your abdomen. Note if you feel hungry or sated. And once you have noticed the organs and muscles of your belly, allow them to relax.

Bring your awareness to your lungs. Feel the air come into and out of them. Note your ribs, and how they move to allow air to enter your body. Become aware of your throat and neck. Allow your awareness to encompass your chin, lips, teeth, tongue, cheeks, nose, jaw, eyes, eyebrows and eyelashes. Let yourself notice your forehead, your hair and finally the top of your head. Now that you are aware of all these parts of yourself, release them so they are present but not uppermost on your mind. Let them float like a delicate lily on a calm, peaceful pond.

Gently bring your attention to your spine. Notice particularly the bottom of your spine, the area known as your tailbone or coccyx. Let that area be particularly relaxed as you begin the next step of your journey.

Bring your awareness from your coccyx to what you are lying upon. Imagine yourself drifting down as you send your awareness through the bed down into the floor below you. Let your awareness go deeper. Picture the floor, and then the base of the building as you go deeper. Then draw your awareness into the foundation and then below it into the earth. Let it delve deeper and deeper still, until your awareness sits in the bedrock itself. Become aware of the solid matter of the rock that cradles us on the earth. It is the stable base on which so much rests.

From this bedrock, envision a thin and beautiful silver vine. Imagine that this vine grows and is held stable by the very earth itself. See it rooted in the rock, the solid bedrock. Imagine it growing, reaching, and stretching up through the soil, past the foundation of the building, past the base of the floor, the floor itself, and up through the place you are lying. See it gently stretch and reach until it finds your tailbone. Allow it to coil gently around your tailbone and pull itself taut delicately. It is now connected both to your tailbone and to the bedrock below. It serves as your anchor, so no matter where you go or what you do, you can remain firmly rooted and centered on the ground. It gives you a sense of stability and peace to know that you are firmly grounded to the solid earth.

This vine coiled around your tailbone will never interfere in what you do or how you live. Its sole purpose is to provide you with support, stability, and foundation. It will give you a constant awareness of the earth around and below you, and as such, it will give you a feeling of being centered and grounded. You can release this vine at any time, and yet you do not need to, since it is only there to help you be your best and most grounded self.

As you lie there and relish this new feeling of being centered and present in your own body, return your awareness to the top of your head. Notice your hair, and how it feels on the crown of your head. Now, bring your awareness to your face, your cheeks, your nose, eyes, eyebrows, and eyelashes. Notice your lips, and note how they feel. Notice your teeth and tongue. Remember them as part of your body. Notice your throat and neck, your shoulders, your upper arms, elbows, forearms, hands, palms, and fingers.

Bring your awareness back up to your shoulders, and feel your spine as you lie there. Notice your chest, and your lungs as they expand and contract with your breath. Note your organs, and your belly, your abdominal muscles, your pelvis, your hips, your genitals, your thighs, your knees, and your calves. Note your feet and appreciate them for connecting you so strongly to the earth. Note your ankles, your soles and your heels, the balls of your feet, and your toes. Remember that you are alive, here on this earth, and you are now connected to it at all times by your choice and by your willingness to be grounded in the here and now.

Note that this journey has been about you finding your center. It has also been about finding a sense of relaxation with your body in the here and now. When you come fully to yourself, you will note that you feel relaxed and peaceful and fully present in your body. When you are ready, come back to your space and open your eyes.

2. Earth Mission: Grow a Seed

Materials:

    Herb seed pack

    Styrofoam cup

    Potting soil sufficient to fill the cup

    Window that faces south on which to keep the cup

This is a long-term Meditative Mission, in that you will take a good bit of time to both prepare and to carry it out. Remember to be patient with yourself. If it does not work the first time you try, keep making the attempt, since it will work, and when it does, you will be filled with the same thrill as the first time you did this task in roughly the sixth grade.

One of the most incredible aspects of getting in touch with the Earth Element is to embark upon one of the great mysteries of life. To many it seems simple, and yet it is a rather miraculous process. What is it that tells a seed to burst open and reach for the warmth of the sun? Something in the earth, or something in the water, or perhaps something in the sun itself that challenges the seed to stretch forth and create something new of itself?

This Mission is about taking a leap of faith. It is about putting something that seems lifeless into the soil, and having faith that new life can come from it. This journey is about finding hope, even when all seems dark.

The soil is dark and might seem lifeless, and yet the soil possesses much life, with billions of microorganisms and bacteria. The soil, which also seems only mineral, is actually also made up of life, air, and water. So things are not as they seem. Remembering this is one of the reasons to take the leap of faith that even when you believe things are their darkest, a turn around a corner might very well bring change and new life.

This journey is a simple one, and yet it is full of the incredible. Choose an herb, perhaps basil or oregano. Purchase a seed pack from your local nursery or perhaps your grocery store. This is best done in the spring, when many stores stock herb seed packs. Next, you can either grab some soil from your backyard if you have one, or you can perhaps purchase or borrow a small amount of potting soil. I believe organic soil is preferred, but it is not strictly necessary. Take a plastic or Styrofoam cup, punch a hole in the bottom (scissors work great for this), and put the cup on a plate. Fill the cup until it is almost full with the potting soil. With one of your fingers, make an indentation in the soil about one-half-inch deep.

As you make the indentation, take a moment to think about the soil and the many miraculous things it does on this planet. It grows our food, and provides us with material for building and for art. It filters waste and purifies our water. It is a truly magnificent part of the earth system. As you think of these things and honor them, remember that the soil is also solid under our feet. This is the material in which you will plant your seeds.

Put a few seeds into the hole you created, and cover the hole with a bit more soil. Breathe deeply while you imagine the seeds being surrounded by the dark, fertile soil. Out of this fertility comes new plant growth, and out of the stability of being grounded in the earth comes our own new growth. Now imagine the seeds sprouting and reaching toward the sun. From now on, tend to the seeds carefully. Nurture them with good sunlight and water. Take responsibility for them, and watch for the new growth. It will happen, and then you can tend to the plant until it is time to harvest it. Tend and nurture its growth just as you might tend and nurture your own growth, of ideas, self-esteem, and self-sufficiency.

If for some reason the seed does not sprout, or if it does sprout but it does not survive, do not judge yourself harshly. This is not about success or failure. Rather, it is about the process of learning to nurture and to accept responsibility for a life. With this acceptance, you will increase your own sense of security because if you can care for a seed, you can care for yourself.

The seed can represent many things. It can represent your own desires, and it can simply represent a seed that needs nurturing.

Honoring the seed is only one way of honoring your own needs for nurturing yourself. To help the seed burst forth and grow into a seedling and then a plant, you need to provide a stable environment and consistent care. These are exactly the same things you need to provide for yourself when you are looking to increase your strength in the Earth Element. You will see that once you have created this environment and appreciated all you can and have provided for this tiny seed, you will also find yourself wanting and providing that for yourself.

This Mission will mirror your own growth as you move forward. You will increase your self-care as you care for the seed. You will take responsibility for yourself even as you take responsibility for the plant you will encourage to grow. When you have succeeded in growing this first plant, you might find you wish to nurture more and more plants. I encourage you to try your hand at gardening on any scale, so you can work with the earth and cultivate it on both the physical and Elemental planes. Please remember to note your feelings in your Life Elements Journal as you care for this seed and make this leap of faith.

3. Earth Mission: Find Your Tree

Many things on our planet can represent the Element of Earth: the fertile soil, mountains, deserts, rocks, crystals, hills, grass, and plants. One of the best representations of the Earth Element is the tree. It can be just about any tree, but it is easy to categorize a tree in the Earth Element for its solid, centered state of being. Trees are stalwart companions. They are rooted deep in the Earth, and they maintain a steady, centered connection to the earth for their entire lives. They grow slowly, and they are incredibly practical. In many ways, a tree can be defined as a closed system. A deciduous tree (one that loses its leaves every winter) loses its leaves in a very practical manner. The leaves fall right near the base of the tree, and as they decompose, they provide nourishment the tree will use in the coming year. This cycle continues year after year in the steady and stable manner so representative of the Earth Element. This stable representative of the Earth Element is what we will seek with the following Mission.

What to do and how to do it

Choose a day with nice weather that is neither too hot nor too cold to complete this Mission. Also, choose a day that will allow you to spend some time outside. You will need to choose an easily accessible location, and one at which you can spend time being relaxed and peaceful. You might wish to go to a park or other place where there are trees in some abundance. You might have to travel a bit to get to your tree, but if you do not, a trip during your lunch hour should suffice beautifully. Please wear walking shoes and dress appropriately for the weather outside. Take an apple with you to give you earth-based sustenance and nourishment as you walk.

Go to a place that is as natural as you can find. Whether it is a school playground or Central Park in New York City, find a natural setting. As you get to the place (and please remember, you might find this tree in your backyard), begin to walk and spend time looking at the trees in your immediate surroundings. Some will be tall and some will be short. Some will be pines, or oaks, or many other species. It is your Mission to look around you and to choose a tree, a good tree. Find one that is beautiful to you. Spend some time and focus on the trees themselves. Notice what thoughts and images come up for you as you study the different trees. Finally, choose a tree that speaks to you in some way.

There might be many reasons a tree will speak to you. You might have a childhood memory surface. Or you might simply like the look of a particular tree without having or needing a reason. It is important that you trust your own instincts here and feel for the support of the earth and environment around you to make your decision. It is that connection between you and all around you, right here and right now, that can help strengthen your Earth Element.

Once you have found your tree, memorize the spot so you know its exact location. And now, take a slow walk. As you put each foot in front of the other, slow and deepen your breathing. Make your inhalations last for four steps, and do the same for your exhalations. Begin to pay close attention to how your feet touch the earth as you walk. Notice if you are touching the ground from your heel first, or if your toes reach out initially. Notice how the earth feels below you. Really feel your feet connect to the ground, step after step.

Now, I want you to begin walking away from the tree, but always keep the tree's exact location planted in the back of your mind. Notice, if you will, if the tree pulls you a little. Your eyes might begin wandering back to the tree, to seek it out and place your attention on its strong presence. In fact, if it does happen, please welcome the sensation; this is a wonderful connection to establish. Allow yourself to meander, and if there are paths to wander, do so. If not, walk around the tree, in a wide circle at first, and then as you walk, decrease the size of your circle so that as you walk, you spiral in toward the tree. Keep your connection to the earth in your steps, and keep alive the feeling of connection between your body and the presence of the tree. After a bit of walking, you will note you are getting closer to the tree, and soon you will be facing the tree.

As you walk, remember to remain aware of how your body feels as it moves. Feel your feet moving forward, one after the other, the muscles of your legs, back, arms, and stomach engaged in the process of propelling you forward as you take each step. Your steps are determined by your will and your thoughts. You provide the anchor of stability that keeps you walking this path, and it is good to give yourself credit for your accomplishment. Feel your body moving, and revel in its strength. Most of us take for granted our bodies' capabilities as we go about our daily lives. It takes an incredible amount of strength sometimes just to get out of bed, particularly if we are not feeling strong that day. Honor that strength within yourself as you walk toward your tree.

This tree also has an incredible amount of strength, and it is that connection—the connection of your strength to the strength of the tree—that we are going to establish today. As you walk, remember the stability that comes from knowing you are stepping solidly on the earth. Walk heel/toe, heel/toe, very gently, and if you have held the apple this whole time, go ahead and eat it. When you are done, please dispose of it properly, and then honor the nourishment the earth has given you. You might wish to say something such as, "I thank the Earth for the bounty in my life."

Continue walking until you return to the tree. Now, step back a bit and look at it. Notice the texture of its bark. Is it smooth, or with knobs on it, or is it rough-hewn? Is the tree large or small? Can you wrap your arms around it and touch your hands on either side of it, or is it too big for that? Notice its height and approximate its size. Then, compare its size to your own to truly sense its proportion and strength.

Now, close your eyes and breathe deeply. Imagine your connection to the soil at your feet as you stand in front of the tree. This connection to the soil through your feet is what can root you to this present moment. If you find it challenging to establish this connection, take a deep breath and see if you can inhale any of the tree's scent. Extend all your senses to acquaint yourself with the tree. Listen for the way the leaves and branches rustle. Gaze at the colors and tones of the bark and leaves. Trust your instincts that you have chosen well. This exercise is as much about learning to trust yourself and your own sense of certainty as it is about getting to know a tree.

When you are ready, put your hands on the tree. Close your eyes and feel the bark. Feel its texture, and in fact push against it, to see how solidly it sits in the earth. It is rooted in the earth below even as it stretches up to the sun, and as you gaze along its length, you might feel a buzzing or a certain amount of vertigo. However, keep holding onto the tree to find stability. Even tiny trees will stay rooted in the earth when they are pushed, because their roots have dug deep and hold centered and stable so the trees might grow.

We too can hold ourselves centered and stable in the earth while we grow. As you stand in front of the tree, imagine its roots curling into and through the soil. Now, imagine your own feet sprouting roots and beginning to dig deep into the earth. Let your roots, your own connection to the earth, hold you stable, centered, and steady on the earth. Imagine your own feet have roots, and you are held stable to the ground. You too can be as centered as this tree. Stand here for a bit and touch the tree. Feel your connection both to your cousin the tree and to the earth below you. That centeredness can be with you at all times. When you wish to establish this connection, simply imagine these same tree roots growing from your own feet. They will ground and center you, so you feel stable and rooted just the like the tree.

If it is an appropriate place, go ahead and sit with your back to the tree. Sit down and feel the tree holding you up, so you can rest against it and know you are protected. The tree provides shade, it provides strength, and it gives us wood so we might build our strong and sturdy houses and also our beautiful violins and guitars and so many other things. It is truly a gift of the earth.

As I stated above, the tree has a very practical yearly cycle. It keeps what it needs close to it, creates its own nourishment, and uses the resources around it, not just to survive, but also to thrive. That practical cycle can also become part of your life. You can set things in motion by taking on the personality of the tree: stalwart, rooted, and grounded. You too can do what needs to be done to ensure you thrive.

The next time you feel overwhelmed, adrift, or overstimulated, allow your memory and imagination to bring you back to this spot, to this place where you feel centered and peaceful. Remember how the sun felt on your face. Remember how the tree felt as it supported you when you leaned against it. The roots you imagined can still be present whenever you need them. You simply have to return to this memory and rekindle the sensation of being rooted into the earth like the tree. Then, when you need to face the challenges of your life, you will approach them from a more stable place because you will be like your cousin, the tree: solid, centered, and grounded, and yet free to reach for the sky. When you are ready, take leave of your tree, but know that this sensation of strength goes with you.

4. Earth Mission: Create a Figurine

Materials:
> Two packets of Sculpey polymer clay (different colors)
> One toothpick
> One glass baking dish (not to be used with food)
> One oven mitt (not to be used with food)
> Rubbing alcohol and cotton balls (to aid in cleanup)

One of Earth Element's most vital characteristics is that it is tangible. We can reach out and find stability and solidity in the Earth Element, from trees to a comfortable chair. Earth's characteristics are touchable and solid. In art, the Elements are neatly divided into four artistic categories. Dance and acting are Fire. Music and painting are Water. Writing and drawing are Air. Sculpture, knitting and woodworking are Earth. To cultivate that artistic Earth quality in ourselves, we will create our own sculpture. We will create a figurine out of a simple building material called Sculpey. Sculpey is a polymer clay, a plastic that is not edible or food-safe. However, it provides an incredibly useful and simple way to create a figurine. You do not need a kiln to fire Sculpey. It can be fired in a regular oven. However, since it is not food safe, please dedicate a baking dish to making things out of Sculpey, and do not use the baking dish for food once you have used it for Sculpey. Once you have begun to make things with Sculpey, I will bet you will want to make more than one thing.

This is an Earth-generating task because it allows you the opportunity to be creative and to make something tangible and physical. The Life Elements website has graphics that will allow you to look at how the figurine might progress, and you can find the images and the directions online. However, just in case you wish to follow your own muse, I have enclosed the written instructions below. Once again, please note I will encourage you to leave judgment out of this Mission. It does not matter whether you are a tremendous sculptor. What matters is that you use the Earth energy within you to create this figurine. Make this a meditative, deliberate process. Allow your stillness to be your guide in the creation of your sculpture. Leave yourself room to have fun, and to make choices and act on those choices from the colors you use to the manner in which you create your unique piece of art. Once you have completed this Mission, your figurine will forever be a tangible symbol of your solid, stable, centered nature. Remember to honor that nature in yourself as you move forward in your growth in the Elements.

In addition to the instructions below, I have provided an online version of this Mission. There are images that correspond to every step of the process. If you wish to view the online version and the included images, please go to: http://www.LifeElements. info/making.htm. Otherwise, please read below, and then have a wonderful time completing this fun and inspiring Mission.

Please note: These instructions can be followed to make a female figurine. If you wish to make a male figurine, you will want to modify some of the instructions. The modification instructions are given a bit later.

Remember: Sculpey is not food safe. Please do not make drinking or eating vessels of any kind out of Sculpey.

1. First, go to a crafts store and purchase two packets of Sculpey in the colors you'd like to use. For this example, I will be using yellows and reds.
2. Break off some of the yellow and work it in your fingers until it becomes rather soft. Do the same with the red, but please note, the red will stain, and so you will want to work the yellow first.
3. Then make a rough cylinder of the yellow and a long "worm" of a small part of the red, and swirl them together. Lay the worm on the yellow cylinder and begin to twist and work the two colors together.
4. Work the colors so they become marbled.
5. Next, roll the entire mass into a ball.
6. Separate the ball into a few pieces
7. Roll one of the bigger pieces into a cylindrical shape. This will be the torso. Roll the other pieces into three spheres and two narrow cylinders.
8. The bigger cylinder other than the torso will be the legs. Cut the piece in half. Shape the separate pieces into legs by flattening one end, making a small bulge in the middle for the knee and flattening the other end for attachment to the torso.
9. Next, cut the smaller cylinder in half to make the arms. Shape the arms by flattening one end to form the hands, and flattening the other end for attachment to the torso.
10. With a toothpick, make hatch marks in the torso for adding the breasts. Attach the breasts.
11. With a toothpick, make hatch marks in the bottom of the torso to prepare it for attaching the legs. Attach a leg to each side of the torso and spread the Sculpey around the legs and torso.

12. Next, attach the arms to the torso, using the same hatching method.

13. Last, attach the head. Remember to make hatch marks on top of the neck, and also to smooth and blend some of the Sculpey of the head onto the torso so the head will be held in place.

If you wish to make a male figurine, do not add the spheres that represent breasts. Instead, use part of one of the spheres to fashion a phallic shape and attach it at the appropriate position using the hatch technique described above. The rest of the instructions remain the same.

14. Find or buy a glass baking dish that you will use only for Sculpey. Preheat the oven to 300 degrees Fahrenheit, and bake for twenty minutes.

15. Remove from the oven promptly and allow the Sculpey figurine to cool before you touch it.

16. Once it has cooled, it will be for you to enjoy. Please remember, though, not to make items from Sculpey that might look they are made to contain food. Sculpey is not food safe, and should be used appropriately.

17. Please also observe appropriate cleaning precautions when working with Sculpey. You will want to soak a cotton ball in rubbing alcohol and clean your hands very well before you wash them clean.

18. The finished figurine is a representation of your creative abilities in the Earth Element. It is something tangible that you will be able to hold and remember your growth and integration. Good for you!

Chapter 17
Fire Missions and Meditations

1. Fire Meditation: Candle Gazing

Materials:
    One candle (white)
    Lighter
    Candleholder
    (Please observe appropriate fire safety precautions.)

Note: If you have Internet connectivity, go to http://www. LifeElements.info. Click the "Meditations" button (the password is "peace" without the quotes) and click the link "Fire Meditation: Candle Gazing."

Sit on the ground, and hold your candleholder in your hands. Breathe deeply for a few minutes and prepare your intention to light the candle. We seldom take the time to think about the incredible process that takes place every time we light a candle. Even if we do not know the chemical reaction occurs, we can still honor the very active process of flame generation.

When you are ready, light your candle and hold it close enough so that your breath moves the flame gently. Note how the wick has darkened as the flame begins to melt the wax. The fire acts on the wax and changes it to a different form as the candle glows. This process of change occurs in us every time we use Fire's energy to be active and creative.

Bring your attention to the flame itself. This is your fire. You created it. As you breathe, the flame moves with you.

Take a moment here to study the flame. We tend to think of candle flames as being yellow; however, as you observe it, you might see that it is actually made up of a number of colors. If your flame is a tall one, you might even notice that all of the colors of the rainbow are represented.

Now, allow the yellow, the most prevalent part of the flame, to draw your attention. It burns as your creativity, yearning to burst free and shower you with its inspirations. Look below the yellow and see the tiny segment of green. This is your center and your growth. This is where the bountiful harvest of your life lies. The growth process in many ways reflects the power and light of fire. Everything must change to grow, and the fire's energy helps those processes take place. Like the energy of the sun, the fire's energy brings heat, growth, and change. Honor the fire's ability to change what it touches, and then let your gaze drop into the blue at the base of the flame. The blue, the higher passion of your secret self, burns brightly. This blue is the gateway to knowledge of self, because below it, barely perceptible, is the violet of your spirit. This is the same spirit that resides within you, and although it guides your actions, inspirations, and ideas, it is barely perceptible day to day. As you watch your flame/spirit, imagine that the violet flame enlarges and envelops the other colors of the fire. Let your spirit enlarge to fill you in the same way. As you inhale, feel your spirit fill you. Let it permeate your fingers, palms, arms, shoulders, head, neck, chest, pelvis, thighs, calves, feet, and toes. Let it have total, conscious control, however briefly, over the flesh form of your body. Let it move through you until you are filled to overflowing with this abundant energy.

Now, breathe with the motion of the flame. As you breathe, let your spirit speak with you. Let it tell you how to proceed on your path, and what your next actions must be. Your spirit knows these truths, and this is your opportunity to learn which passions to follow. Listen well as you learn your next steps on the journey.

Honor yourself for the communion you have just achieved. Find peace in the knowledge that when you follow your spirit's guidance, you are actively working for your highest good, and although you might not be consciously aware of this spirit part of you daily, you can be certain it exists and acts on your behalf. Now, allow it to recede slowly from every secret part of you. Begin to feel the sensations that have not been so present in your body. Relax into the form you have known for so long. As you watch the flame, see the violet begin to recede from the other colors in the candle. It will leave a little of itself behind in every color, as your spirit will leave a little of itself behind in every part of you. Feel it leave the yellow, and now the green. As it recedes from the blue, feel it mix with the blue and flow downward to re-form as the base of the flame and the base of your being.

You have met what guides you in your innermost dreams. This is the part of you that spurs you into action. This is the spark of passion, action, and creation. Know that you can access this part of yourself whenever you have need. This passionate spark will propel you forward into your life.

2. Fire Mission: Act of Creation

Materials:

One skein of yarn

Certainly, if we look at the First Law of Thermodynamics, we see that all energy is already present. Energy can be transferred from one system to another, but it cannot be created or destroyed.[2] Matter can change form, but energy remains the same. Fire is the agent of this kind of change quite often. Fire can burn wood and turn it into its basic state of carbon. Fire takes something and changes it to create something new. That is what honoring and building fire is all about—making change to create something new. Here, we will also take a certain material and act upon it to create something that did not exist before. Certainly the raw materials have existed, but we will take those raw materials and make something new from them. Your creative spirit is always there, and this Mission invites that spirit to come and play.

This Fire Element generator is subtle, and it will make changes in you, most particularly if you take the time truly to honor the fact that you will be the creator of something that did not previously exist.

This act of creation is a simple one, but it is one with which you can see concrete results. You will need a skein of yarn in a color you like. We are going to do finger knitting. Now, most of the time when people think of knitting, they think of making something that is practical. Today, we are not here to make something practical. We are simply here to go through the process of creation.

Once you have bought or chosen your yarn, find the end of it. If you have never used yarn before, the end is often found in the center of the rounded ends. Feel inside the center hole to locate the end of the yarn and pull out a few feet. Take approximately twelve inches from the end and hold it in between your thumb and index finger. For a moment, study the yarn in its current state. Notice the length of it, and test its strength by pulling on it gently. Take note of its overall shape. It should generally have a straight, somewhat soft, malleable shape (unless you chose a specialty yarn, in which case, please note how that yarn feels). Bring your awareness to where it is now, and maintain your awareness as you consciously exert your will and your physical motion to change the yarn.

While you will not change its basic essence, you will, through the application of your will and actions, modify its shape. Now, using your right hand, wind the yarn around the fingers of your left hand, starting from the spot between your thumb and forefinger. Start by winding the yarn over your index finger, then under your middle finger, over the ring finger, and then under and around the pinky finger. *Please note, if you want to see a video depicting the winding process, go to the Life Elements website: http://LifeElements. info/Missions.htm, and click "Video for the Fire Mission: Act of Creation."*

From this point, keep winding, but this time go under the ring finger, over the middle finger, and under and around the index finger.

From here, go one more time, and this time go under the middle finger, over the ring finger, and under and around the pinky.

Go one more time under the ring finger, and then over the middle finger. This time, however, stop before you get to the index finger and let the yarn hang between the index and middle fingers. See Figure 2.

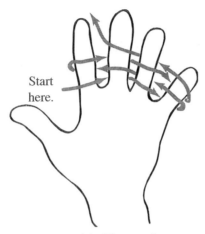

Figure 2. This illustration
depicts the first step in the
winding process on the left
hand palm side up.

Once the yarn has been wound, leave the yarn that is attached to the skein between your forefinger and middle finger. Now, grasp the yarn at the bottom of your pinky finger and flip it over the yarn at the top of your pinky (leave that yarn on your finger) and off the finger all together. Do the same thing for the yarn on your ring finger.

Now, flip the yarn off the middle finger and then flip it from your forefinger. Once that has been accomplished, you will note that you now have a row of yarn still left on your hand. To continue to build the chain you have started creating, you will need to wind on the second row.

Start with the yarn between your index and middle finger, and wind it in back and around to the front of your index finger. From here, go under the middle finger, over the ring finger, and under and around the pinky finger.

Go one more time under the ring finger and then over the middle finger. This time, however, stop before you get to the index finger and let the yarn hang between the index and middle fingers. (See Figure 3.) This will once again leave you with two rows of yarn on all of your fingers.

Repeat the previous steps to pull the yarn and flip it over and off your fingers. Remember to pull it off the pinky finger, and then work your way over until you reach the index finger. Repeat the winding and flipping approximately thirty more times.

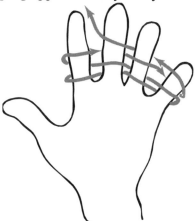

Figure 3. Ongoing steps of
the winding process.

Very quickly, you will notice you are creating a chain. Tug on the bottom of the chain to elongate it properly so you can clearly see the results of your efforts.

The key here is to appreciate the change in status of whatever you make. It starts out as a long, straight string, but when you act on it, you change its existence. While it retains its essence as yarn, it has now been changed by your action to be a stronger, more solid, and more beautiful rope.

3. Fire Mission: Dance

Materials:
> Three or four songs you love on CD or computer
> A CD player or some other device to play these songs
> Fifteen minutes of undisturbed alone time
> Fun scarves (optional)

The Fire Element relates most closely with the body's motion. Electrical impulses along the nervous system spark our muscles, tendons, bones, and ligaments, and make us move. The passion for something is what urges us onward.

Thus, it is Fire's nature to be in motion—to do and to act. Since Fire governs motion, one of the best ways to generate and honor Fire in our lives is to move our bodies. There are few better ways to do that than to dance.

This Mission will take you on a quest to getting to know your body a bit. You will need to find a song you absolutely adore. It does not have to be a stereotypical dance piece. A popular misconception is that only certain types of music can be dance music. That is simply not true. Most songs can be used as dance music, and we are going to do just that. One of the things I have discovered in the course of integrating Fire into my life is that almost any piece of music can become a dance piece if the person listening allows his or her body to move to the rhythm of the song.

Choose a song that is perhaps three to five minutes in length. Find a time you will not be disturbed for at least fifteen minutes. I recognize this might be challenging for some. If you share your home with others, you can easily do this entire exercise while wearing headphones.

This Mission will access the Fire Element by getting you into your body and moving. You will engage your inner dancer, and you will get the opportunity to connect, perform, and move. I recognize that for some, this might be challenging, and I encourage you to do it anyway. One of the things that happens as we get older is we begin to lose the ability simply to be in our bodies. As we age and grow we begin to use our minds, sometimes to the exclusion of being present in our bodies. Thus, the freedom we felt as children to run and be free take a backseat to thoughts, ideas, and practical concerns. This Mission is all about rediscovering that sense of motion and dance. Here we go!

We all have a favorite song or two. These are songs that speak to us somehow. It does not matter whether they are fast or slow. The only thing that matters about them is that we love them. What is/are your songs? List at least four of them in your Life Elements Journal. (Note: if you have trouble finding songs, I have placed a piece called "Fire Dance" on the Life Elements website at: http://LifeElements. info/Missions.htm. Feel free to download it and play it as your first piece. It will inspire you to find other music as well.) Find them on

CD or make them somehow readily accessible to you. This exercise will use these songs to help you open yourself to the incredible ways in which your body can move. You will begin to see your body's strength, flow, and flexibility as you open to the passionate dance of Fire.

Find a time when you will not be disturbed, and put on some comfortable, easy-to-move-in clothing. This Mission does not require more than approximately fifteen minutes for the first time you complete it. After you try it once, you might find you want more time to explore the way your body moves.

Lower the lights in your room. Sit down on the floor and turn on the first of the songs on your list. As the song begins to play, close your eyes and listen to it. Listen closely to the beat and cadence of the piece. Each piece of music has a kind of pulse. See if you can identify that pulse as you listen to the song.

Once you feel you have the pulse, bring your awareness to your non-dominant hand (if you are right-handed, bring your awareness to your left hand and vice versa). Focus on that hand, and as you feel the pulse of the song, begin to move or flex your fingers in time to the pulse. Once the fingers are moving, add your wrist and the rest of your hand and let it move to the song. You might even begin to move more than just your lower arm. The rest of your arm might "get into the act" as you lose yourself in the pulse of the song. Let your imagination run free while you move your hand in circles or spirals, or however the music moves you. Do this until the end of the song.

You might wish to put the same song on again, so you can continue to play with its cadence, or you might wish to move on to the next song. Regardless, put a song on again, sit on the floor, and once again engage your non-dominant hand to begin to move to the rhythm of the music.

This time, as your hand begins to move, see if you can incorporate the other hand into the act as well. Let it begin to undulate in rhythm with the other hand. Let them dance around each other or in concert with one another. If you feel inspired, you might wish to move your entire upper body. Let yourself move and flow as you let your body respond to the cadence of the music. If you feel even more inspired, you might wish to stand up and begin to move to the song.

Keep focusing on your hands and let them move. Let them guide the rest of your body to synch up with the song and move to it. Let yourself play. Become a ballerina, and joyfully spin or pirouette. Or you might be a Broadway dancer, or a hip-hop artist, whichever resonates the best with you. However you dance, let the movement come from your hands, and once you are comfortable with that, see if you can move your awareness of motion to your belly. Let your center be what begins to guide your dance, and allow yourself to enjoy it!

You might find you end up dancing to all four songs. I encourage you to keep going until you feel finished. Once you are done, sit for a moment and quietly acknowledge to yourself what you have accomplished. Some people might feel awkward when beginning to dance. Although that might happen, I encourage you to complete the Mission anyway. The awkward feeling is the natural ignition of the Fire Element. It is a growing pain, if you will. Once you become more comfortable with the motion of your body in space, your awkwardness will cease and you will simply enjoy the motion and energy of the dance.

I encourage you to repeat this Mission often. There are so many benefits to moving your body in this way, and you will find you really come to delight in dancing. Once again, I urge you not to judge yourself on the quality of your dancing. This is simply an opportunity to move, dance, and feel good about your body. Be creative. Wear fun clothes the next time you do this. Or, if you have swaths of fabric, you might want to use them as veils and move like a belly dancer or someone from one of the "Tales of the Arabian Nights." This is just for you. Be sinuous. Be sensual. Be energetic. Dance. Then, write down your reactions and feelings on a separate page of your Journal.

Do this Mission at least once a week to keep increasing your Fire energy. Put a date before each entry so you will see how your Fire energy progresses as you dance more and more.

4. Fire Mission: A Grand Adventure

Materials:

    Markers

    Blank paper

    Magazines

    Scissors

    Glue or tape

As you might have learned from the previous Mission, one of the best ways to cultivate the Fire Element is to move your body. I believe each one of us has an internal passion. Some, those who are already strong in the Fire Element, have little trouble letting their inner passionate nature come out in their daily lives. They are able to move in the world as extremely creative, fiery individuals. Some of us, most especially those of us who are more Earth-oriented people, might have some challenges and obstacles to moving in the world like a burning flame. However, even if we have challenges in that arena, we can still explore and encourage that passionate side of ourselves. This Mission will help you bring out your inner passionate nature.

Here, I will ask you to set aside some time so you can go on an adventure. It does not have to be big. It can be anything you do by and for yourself. Adventures, by their natures, require some daring behavior, and this is extremely characteristic of Fire energy. Now is the time to access your courage and take a leap of faith in your own spirit of adventure. We all have one, even if it is hidden in some of us. It is of vital importance to begin to access that spirit in yourself so you can move forward in your life on your own terms.

Some people find this particular Mission extremely challenging because as a whole, we tend to want to have company on our adventures, and those who are especially Earth-oriented might be daunted by the idea of striking out for an adventure at all. It is hard to contemplate doing things on our own or without support. However, that is the very reason to cultivate this aspect of ourselves. If we do take an adventurous step forward, it opens us up to many other possibilities, because we address our fears about being alone while still being free to be adventurous and/or spontaneous.

Take some time right now and write out a fantasy adventure in your Life Elements Journal. If you could go anywhere or do anything, what would it be? Flesh it out in as much detail as you can. Where would you go? How would you get there? What are the kinds of things you would need to take with you? Who might you meet? What might you see?

Once you have it written out, take some time and copy your adventure onto a blank piece of paper, decorate it with pictures or your own drawings of the place, and then hang the paper up somewhere. Let it serve as a reminder of the adventure of your dreams. Remind yourself that someday your adventure might indeed be possible.

In the meantime, let us look at an adventure you might have right now. Take some time and peruse the suggestions below. Or, if you have an idea for a starter adventure, perhaps you can do that. It is now time to choose your adventure and go on it. If you are feeling particularly adventurous, go on a trip somewhere. Go to a new city or country even. I know this is dreaming big, but if it is possible and you feel up to it, then the world is really your oyster. Certainly, you will want to plan an adventure such as this out a bit, but that can be part of the fun. If that is more than you wish to do for now, here are some other possible adventures that will keep you closer to home as you begin this process.

Go to the movies alone. Take the time and simply do it. Choose a movie you wish to see and go by yourself and enjoy it as fully as possible. You can plan which movie you will see, or if you want a real mini-adventure, choose a movie at random that happens to be playing when you go to the theater. Afterward, see how you feel, and then write your reactions in your Life Elements Journal. You might notice some negative feelings crop up, and you want nothing more than to go back home where things feel more comfortable. However, you might also notice you simply had fun. This might even begin a new habit for you. I do this quite often, and I call it my afternoon movie time.

You can go dancing. Put on your favorite "fun outfit" and head over to any one of the places that teach ballroom dancing for an hour or so before the opening dancing that takes place for the rest of the evening. This will happen more often in urban areas, but you might be surprised how many churches and synagogues hold dances in your area.

Put on your favorite outfit and go to a bar or pub. Once there, strike up conversations with people just to talk and have fun. There need be no other motivation than to make fun connections with people. In some ways, it is a role you don for the evening. You will behave as the outgoing, vivacious person you wish to become, and you might be surprised to find it is even easier than you thought.

If you find some of these adventures too daunting, then first ask a friend to come with you and help you accomplish some of these adventures. Then, when you feel more confident, you can complete some of them on your own.

Take the time to do these adventures and really allow yourself to enjoy them as much as possible. This Mission will do an incredible amount to cultivate your inner Fire. We are all made up of all four Elements. It is just that some are more prevalent in us to begin with. Once you begin these smaller adventures and they are successful, I believe you will find it easier and more exciting to have grander ones. You will gain greater confidence in both your ability and your desire to complete your own adventures. As you feel more inclined to try more things on your own, go ahead and do them. Remember to be safe and to have fun as you open yourself to your passionate life.

Chapter 18
Water Missions and Meditations

1. Water Meditation: Cup of Wonder

Materials:

The loveliest or most meaningful bowl, cup, glass, or goblet you own

Water in a pitcher (Sufficient water to overfill the cup)

Plastic container that can hold the bowl or cup and water overflow

Small bead or pebble

Larger pebble

Pen

Piece of paper (standard size)

Note: If you have Internet connectivity, go to http://www. LifeElements.info. Click the "Meditations" button (the password is "peace" without the quotes) and click the link "Water Meditation: Cup of Wonder."

This exercise can be done in the house, or if possible, it would be terrific to do it outside. Do this exercise in the early evening, if possible, just around twilight.

First, slowly fill a pitcher with water. Then, take the most beautiful or meaningful bowl or cup you own and put it inside the plastic container. Put all of these things onto a table or on the floor near a window. Sit by them and get comfortable. Take in a few deep breaths to prepare for this exercise. Now, spend a minute looking at the water in the pitcher. See if you can note and also appreciate how as the pitcher was filled, the water flowed to take up every bit of available space inside it. Water flows to fill the empty spaces.

Keep that thought of flowing to fill the empty space in your mind as you close your eyes. In your mind's eye, imagine yourself becoming fluid. See yourself flowing like the water in the pitcher. Feel what it would feel like to be so fluid and able to adapt to what surrounds you. If you were the water in the pitcher, you might find yourself flowing to fill every curve and dimension of that pitcher. You would move easily where you are taken, and you would still retain your own identity, even while contained in the pitcher. See if you can be conscious of what it truly means to adapt yourself to whatever space you inhabit and also to be peaceful in that adaptation. Water flows into the available spaces, and then settles so its surface is smooth. In a similar fashion, strong emotions can create new spaces in us, and once we can handle those strong emotions, we can allow ourselves to become peaceful, while at the same time we feel our emotions truly and authentically.

Allow yourself to experience the sights and sounds of the evening. Feel the evening against your skin, and know that the water in your container is naturally connected to all around you. Now take a deep breath and say the words, "As this water is connected to all that surrounds it, so am I connected to all that surrounds me."

Allow your connection to both the water and your surroundings to deepen as you breathe gently and fully. Find and keep the peaceful place the water occupies as it lies in the pitcher. As you feel this connection, slowly lift the pitcher and with conscious thought, slowly pour the water into your bowl until it is two-thirds full. As you do so, notice and stay aware of how the water moves from one receptacle to the other. It fluidly changes to fit its new environment while it retains its identity. Eventually, the water settles into a state of peace, and it is only agitated when something acts on it. Its natural state while in this container is to be quiet and peaceful.

Sit quietly, take a few deep breaths, and then look into the bowl. Allow the water to calm so it is still. If you see your own reflection, let the face you see be at peace. Consciously release your face and soften your eyes by gently closing and then opening them. Look into the bowl again, and see if you can relax your forehead and eyebrows. If you are used to gritting your teeth or clenching your jaw, let them go gently slack as well.

Now, look at the water again and notice, if you will, that the water fills all of the available space. Everywhere it can flow, it flows. Everything it can fill, it fills. It flows to take on and fill the shape of whatever contains it. What does this mean to us?

Let us examine and compare water and our emotions. Our emotions are ever changeable. We have already seen that we can move from one emotion to the next with relative and sometimes surprising speed. When we are happy, our happiness appears to know no bounds. It expands to encompass all that is around us and spills over onto others. The same can be said when we are sad. Our sorrow can seem to be a bottomless, murky well of despair. This same changeability applies to water A calm sea can become a furious flood. Or it can be the raging thunderstorm of anger. It can be the soothing serenity of an autumn rain after the heat and intensity of summer. It can be the sorrow of ocean depths, and it can be the joyful play of the waves against the shore. Both our emotions and Water have the capability of infinite change and growth, and they are more closely related than many of us understand. This means that water and emotion both are ever expanding. We can use our emotional center to expand, to love, and to express our emotions fully and authentically.

Now, look at the bowl. Allow yourself to be at peace and serene. As you sit with the water, you might notice you begin to get certain thoughts and ideas. Write down these thoughts and ideas in your Journal. Most particularly write down your feelings if you experience them as you look calmly into the water. Breathe deeply.

Imagine your heart is like the water in this bowl. It is contained, and yet it can expand beyond that which contains it. Like the water, your heart can fill all around it with love and acceptance. As you wander in your mind's eye, note what you feel. If you feel a certain amount of apprehension while doing this exercise, please acknowledge the apprehension. We are here in this place, together, to honor whatever emotions arise from looking into the bowl and from accessing your heart's depth.

If you do feel a sense of apprehension or even silliness, please give yourself permission to really feel, and then let those feelings flow out of you and into the cup. Taking time to honor yourself is a wonderful thing to do, and while you might feel awkward, simply acknowledge the awkward feelings and then imagine them flowing out of you and into the water. This might occur more than once while you are doing this exercise, and it is just fine. Each time it happens, simply let those emotions flow into the cup, and in your imagination, allow the cup to accept them. Eventually, you will have released sufficient tension and awkward feelings into the cup, all that will be left are the more peaceful and positive emotions of acceptance. This is the point at which you can look into the cup and allow your own face to reflect back to you the love and self-acceptance you can now promise to yourself. Say the words, "I love and honor myself and the fluidity of my emotions."

Very gently, drop the small pebble into the center of the bowl. Notice what happens to the water. Did the pebble create waves? How quickly did they abate and the water settle once again?

Now, drop in the larger pebble. Notice the water's reaction and the waves that are created. Once again, though, they settle and the water becomes still. These pebbles are like new emotional stimuli that come into our lives. Some are small, and while they do affect our lives, we recover and quickly come back to emotional equilibrium. Others are larger, and it can take longer to return to a balanced emotional state. Regardless, all are part of our experience, and we can incorporate them into our lives. These stimuli change our emotional states. It does not matter whether or not we recognize these changes, but everything that affects us changes us permanently, even if it only does so in minute ways. Either it reinforces what we already knew, or it brings to us a new sense of being and feeling.

When the pebbles dropped into the water, they changed everything in that water. Despite the fact that the water eventually settled down to its normal still state, everything inside was different because of these new stimuli. None of the molecules of water in that bowl will ever be in the same place again, and although the water remains contained and although the water remains water, it is now different. It is a wonderful idea to honor those new stimuli, because they do indeed bring us new experience and a new emotional landscape every day.

When the pebbles hit the water, the water rebounded and waves radiated and moved in the bowl until the water settled again. That radiating feeling is the same feeling that occurs when we accept ourselves and arrive at a place of self-love. This is the same kind of expanding emotional center created when our hearts are at peace. We can have this in our bodies, and in our lives.

Take a moment to sit quietly as you gaze into the center of the bowl. Listen and learn from seeing the center of the water, and the center of your emotions. I will give you a few minutes to spend time in this very safe place. Honor the thoughts and feelings that come up for you, and write them down so you can have greater awareness of and access to them in the future.

In this exercise, you found and acknowledged both negative and positive emotions. You have allowed the water in the bowl to contain your feelings of awkwardness or sadness. Now, you must acknowledge that those feelings will be a part of you, but you can also experience them, express them, and hold them when it is necessary for you to do so. The first and most important part of this is to give yourself sufficient time to feel, identify, and acknowledge your emotions before you act on them. This extra bit of time spent figuring out exactly what you feel will yield tremendous results in maintaining equilibrium in your emotional state. In other words, the more time we spend feeling our emotions, the easier it will become to express them in a way that they are easier for others to hear.

Often, we simply react to emotions, but just as often that means we are not truly dealing with them or expressing them authentically. You might wish to repeat this Water Mission a number of times, since each time you do it, it will give you space and time to feel, and to acknowledge what you feel. Then, with time, you will be able to move through your emotional life without the many land mines that occur when you react without first acknowledging what is really going on internally. The entirety of your emotions will remain a part of you, and yet they are nothing you cannot feel and manage.

Take the bowl in both your hands. Hold it up at eye level and say the words, "I accept all of my emotions as being a part of me. Both the negative and the positive are all a part of who I am. I do not deny them, and will endeavor to feel them truly and express them authentically."

As you do this, allow those words to sink deep inside you. Let them sit in your center, as if you are the bowl that contains them. This new awareness of your own feelings will eventually make them more available to you as you progress. You will feel and express yourself from the authentic place

Now, pour the water into your plastic container. When you are able, you will pour it onto the ground outside. When you do so, imagine the water flowing down into the groundwater, returning to be a part of the greater earth community and universal emotion.

Pour the last of the water in the pitcher into your bowl. You will now take the water into yourself. This is symbolic of owning all of your emotions. Many say you should not allow yourself to feel your negative emotions, but I believe that since they remain a part of you, they must be integrated into the whole of who you are right now. Thus, if you have negative emotions, it is best to acknowledge and manage them rather than to negate or ignore them.

Take the bowl in both hands once again. Slowly lift the bowl to your lips and take a sip of the water into your mouth. Let the water sit in your mouth. Be aware of how it feels rolling around your tongue. Notice how the water fills every available space in your mouth. It can wash your mouth clean, and it can quench your thirst. Swirl the water around as if you were drinking a fine wine. Get the water's taste in your mouth. Make sure that your entire mouth is wet from the water, and when you are ready, slowly, deliberately, swallow the water. Note any feelings that arise from having swallowed the water. When you are ready, take two more sips in that same reverent way and honor the water that has quenched your thirst.

Take the water in the plastic container outside and find a tree or plant on which to pour the water. Begin by gently tipping the container to let the water slowly pour out. All the while, say these words: "Water, I thank you for quenching my thirst, and I honor the earth and this tree (or plant) by quenching its thirst."

Now, go back home and relax into your new emotional freedom and expression. At first it might feel slightly uncomfortable, and your feelings might feel like clothes that do not fit well. Try to breathe into what is happening to you, and write down the feelings and thoughts that come to you. Your Life Elements Journal will be especially important in this way. It will provide you with a place to organize and recognize your feelings and how they are a part of you. Please note: This sometimes creates great changes in people, so you will want to be extra kind and gentle with yourself as you move forward in this process.

Repeat this Mission as often as you feel the need. It is always of benefit to acknowledge and express your emotions authentically.

2. Water Mission: Make Music

I believe that our connection with music is a part of and gives us access to some of our oldest and deepest emotions. Lullabies, for example, are used in one form or another to bond parent and child. Parents sing to their children to calm them, to connect with them, and to express their love for them. As babies, many of us heard lullabies, and that connection between music and love was firmly established. Music can and has made a deep impact, whether or not it is something of which we are conscious day to day. We intuitively react to music, and many of us have favorite songs that affect our moods, make us joyful, and might even inspire us to dance.

Although the appreciation of music is a wonderful activity, this Water Mission will be slightly more active in its relationship to music. I will ask you to make music: to reach deep inside and bring forth sound and melody. You will create the music, and you will be moved by your own creation.

While some people make music a mathematical exercise, I believe in approaching it from a more intuitive standpoint. There is much to be learned from developing a connection: an intuitive connection with music. Studies have shown that music can have a profound effect on our emotional state of being. Music can lift spirits, and it can propel us into feelings of immense joy and contentment. When we hear a favorite song, our mood can be altered. The feelings music elicits are in many ways the key to developing our emotions so we can then later access them more easily.

Many people know they are feeling emotions, but they are not capable of discerning those emotions. They might also be challenged to be honest with themselves or others about what they feel in the moment. They react emotionally, but without a true foundation of knowledge about the extent or quality of their emotions. Therefore, they find themselves acting out or lashing out rather than acknowledging their emotions and working from a centered heart.

This is where music can help guide us to our emotional core. Since so many of us were exposed to music as babies, it can resonate with us on the primal level. However, since we all had unique experiences with it, it will influence each of us differently. We all come to music, our appreciation of it and participation in it, from different perspectives. Some of us played musical instruments as children. Some of us sang in choirs in school or in church. Further, some of us were given the message that we did not have that particular talent, and we were told to stop singing or playing. Others never had the opportunity to make music, and were relegated to the sidelines. We all had different reactions to our experience of music. In many ways, the manner in which we were treated with respect to music back then informs and even dictates how we react to it now.

Therefore, I ask you now to remember. Go back to your first memory of music. It might have been in music class. Or, if someone in your family sang or played an instrument, you might have had exposure in that manner. Close your eyes and place yourself back in that space. Remember your age. Remember the surroundings. Take the time to flesh out this memory, and create the scene for yourself as you return to that space. How did it feel to hear music? How was music being made? Was it someone you knew, or did you first hear the music on the radio, or a record or tape or CD? Was it instrumental, or were there voices raised in song? Go back and rediscover what it felt like to hear music the first time. Identify your feelings as best you can, and write them in your Life Elements Journal.

Now, I will ask you to close your eyes and go back and remember the first time you created music. We have all tried in one way or another to make music. Some of us showed talent and were encouraged, or were sometimes required to practice instruments or sing. Many children lugged heavy instruments to and from school when they were growing up. Some of us had challenges in music class, because we had special needs with respect to learning music or singing. Unfortunately, teachers often relegated those students with special needs to the arena of "can't be helped," and those students' musical interests and abilities were stunted if not downright obliterated.

Remember what you felt about music and most especially making music and rediscover what it felt like to make music. Remember the feeling of using an instrument, whether or not it was your voice, to create sound that could be shared with others. Some of you might have happy memories; others might have difficult or challenging ones. Regardless of which they are, please attempt to connect with that young person and reassure him or her that this sharing of music and sound was welcome and beautiful regardless of what anyone else said or did. After all, they do not call it "making a joyful noise" for nothing.

We were all born to make music and sound, and it is now time to reclaim that ability and desire. Behind your closed eyes, keep remembering what it felt like to make music. Acknowledge what you felt, whether it was positive or less than positive, and try to sit with that feeling. This might be challenging to do, but it is one of the best ways to open ourselves to our "heart homes." It is when we truly acknowledge what we feel and really allow ourselves to experience some of these emotions that we can access some of our most deeply buried feelings. Most particularly, if your experience of making music ended with you feeling somehow diminished or sad, you might find this Mission is especially powerful and brings up some deep emotions. Attempt to truly feel your emotions about your memories. They are a part of both your past and your present, and they will inform how you feel and how you move forward.

Write your experience of these memories in your Life Elements Journal, take a moment to breathe, and come to a sense of peace with where you are now. Then please continue.

While we can acknowledge that music can create an internal space for free expression of emotion, few of us consciously turn to music to help alleviate sadness or access happier emotions. Fewer of us think of creating music as an access point to our emotions. In part, this might be because many of us are raised without music in our homes. Or, we might have had interest in music, but that interest was belittled or ignored. If an interest in music was ignored, then we likely did not have an opportunity to create music. Without the expression of feelings that listening to music or making music can bring, many of us live our lives with a crucial piece missing. This Mission is designed to help you establish a connection with music, and as such, with an intimate, emotional part of you. In particular, if you come from a background that rejected music or musical pursuits, this Mission will open new vistas for you. You will discover new musical and emotional realms. *Note: To complete this Mission, you will need to have Internet access. Please go to http://LifeElements. info and click the "Missions" button. Then, see the "Sing" Mission under Water Missions for the appropriate audio files.*

Since many of us do not have musical instruments readily available, we will use the oldest musical instrument: the voice. Singing gives us the closest possible connection to the Water Element because there is such incredible intimacy inherent in using our bodies to create sound and music. You will use your very cells, blood, muscles and bones to create the vibrations that make the song. I recognize that you might have fear associated with singing, and I will help you overcome any fear and get you singing. We will prepare to sing and start slowly to keep you as comfortable as possible with this intimate and revolutionary process.

I believe singing should be an Olympic sport. Just like an athlete uses his or her entire body to run, or play a sport, a singer uses his or her entire body to sing. We use the muscles and bones in our torso, legs, shoulders, lungs, the cavities in our bodies, and our breath to sing. So, just as marathon runner would never dream of running without warming up, we will not sing without first preparing ourselves to do so. So, first, let's warm up. Note: Please listen to your body and do nothing that might injure you in any way.

Warm-ups (To be done before every time you sing)

1. March in place (Two minutes) Singing uses muscles that must be warmed up in order to function at their peak.
2. Prepare the body to maintain a column of air ("Prepare Neck, Torso, and Lungs" track 2 on the website)
   a. Shoulder roll (Five rolls in each direction)

   b. Half neck roll (Left side to front to right side and back)
   c. Half neck roll to the back
   d. Neck stretch (Turn neck to the side and stretch and then for a deeper stretch turn chin down to the shoulder)
   e. Arms above head stretch (Lift both arms and stretch the right arm up lengthening your ribs and then follow with the left arm)
   g. Alternate making your face really small and big to stretch and limber up the facial muscles.
   h. Horse noise. Put your lips together and lightly engage the muscles around them. Take in a deep breath and blow out through your mouth while you keep your lips compressed.
   i. Yawn with "Ah" sound
3. Posture (Stand to sing so you can keep an uninterrupted column of air)
   a. Practice standing to sing. Stand with both feet shoulder width apart, your knees slightly bent and your spine straight. Lightly tug up the hair at the very top of your head. Jaw is loose and breathing is relaxed.

4. Deep breathing correctly. ("Deep Breathing" Track 3 on the website) Your stomach is relaxed and flowing out on inhalation. Your ribs are relaxed and expanding and your shoulders are relaxed and down. (You'll find when you sing that [usually because of nervousness] your shoulders start to ride up and get tense around your neck. Consciously lower and relax them whenever you notice this.
   a. Inhale and exhale full deep breath five times.
   b. Inhale a full, deep breath using good technique and exhale on a whispered "Ah" five times. Horse noise is great for finding where you are using your breath.
   c. Inhale and then exhale on a low "Mmm" five times.
   d. Inhale and exhale on a "Ah" sound.
   e. Yawn a "Ah" sound five times.
5. Make a tone on a vowel. When you sing, remember to open your mouth sufficiently wide so that you can put the tips ·of two of your fingers between your front teeth. This will ensure

that you get the best quality sound. Note: Some people have a challenge in singing the correct notes or pitches when they sing. Most often, this means they need to develop a specific listening skill to match the pitch they are trying to sing. The best way to match the pitch you hear is to time to listen to the note, imagine yourself singing and then open your mouth and sing. ("Tones on a Vowel" Track 4 on the website).

    a.   Ah (Follow the "Two-finger Rule" for all of these.)

    b.   Eh

    c.   Ee

    d.   Oh

    e.   Ooh

    f.   Ah, Eh. Ee, Oh, Ooh (on one note)

6. Sing with adding consonants ("Tones With Consonants" Track 5 on the website)

    a.   mah meh mee moh moo (nah, tah, lah, sah, kah, etc.). Practice all exercises with different consonants.

7. Practice tongue twisters to develop control of the muscles in and around your mouth. ("Minimal animal" on the website)

    a.   Minimal animal develops facility of the lips and tongue.

Now that you have warmed up, we will sing a song. Click the "Sing and Rejoice" link on the website and let's join together in song. The lyrics are simple yet beautiful. They are:

Sing and rejoice
Sing and rejoice
Let all things living
Sing and rejoice

You may feel nervous as you embark on this and I encourage you to take a deep breath and plunge into singing with your whole heart. After all, that is what this is all about. We are here to open our hearts and access our emotional centers. Singing will be one of the best ways to accomplish this sacred task. Please do not judge yourself harshly on your singing. With a bit of time and practice, you will only improve, I promise you. Simply remember to stand or sit up straight, breathe deeply, use the two-finger rule and sing.

Note any of your feelings in your Life Elements Journal. If you want to try a second song, please click the "Rose" link and join me in another song. The words are:

> Rose, Rose, Rose, Rose
> Shall I ever see thee wed?
> I shall marry at my will, Sire
> At my will."

Practice these songs as often as you like and enjoy the music you make. It will bring you much happiness. If you find that you want to bring even more music into your life, click the "Make music with an instrument" link and follow the instructions for that special online Mission. Note: You will need a recorder for that Mission.

3. Water Mission: Explore and Acknowledge Your Emotions

With this Mission, we will identify and accept our emotions. Before you do anything else, fill a glass with water. Then, take your Journal and turn to a blank page. Write out the sentence phrases below. You will then complete the sentences with experiences from your life.

Some of your answers might make you uncomfortable, because this Mission asks you to acknowledge your feelings, both good and bad, and then to feel them no matter what they might be. Sometimes we want to run away from our feelings, especially if they make us uncomfortable. This Mission will ask you to go in depth, to become aware of exactly what you feel about one thing.

As mentioned, write the following phrases in your Life Elements Journal. Then, complete them with something from your own life experience. Remember, you might access intense emotions. Try to breathe through them until you feel calm again. (This is an excellent way of bringing the Air Element into your life and combining it with Water to help you move through your life.)

First, complete each sentence, and then you will spend a bit of time accessing how you feel about what you have just written. Write about your feelings. As you identify them on paper, they will become easier to see and acknowledge.

I love . . .
I like it when . . .
I enjoy . . .
I feel jealous of . . .
I dislike it when . . .
I feel envious of . . .
I feel wonderful when . . .
I feel sad if . . .
I feel entitled to . . .
I am irritated by . . .
I feel happy when . . .
I feel unhappy when . . .
I feel giddy when . . .
I feel frustrated by . . .
I am angry at . . .
I am pleased when . . .
I feel mad when . . .
I feel lonely when . . .
I get agitated if . . .

Now that you have completed the statements, take the time to be honest about how you feel about them. Some will affect you more than others. Choose the three that give you the strongest and most positive reaction. Reread what you have written for them. Then, take the time to really feel what you feel about them. Get in depth into your feelings. Identify what you feel. See if you can put a name to the emotion. Study it as if you are a scientist who is trying to uncover a deep mystery. Then go deeper, and see if you can figure out what causes the feeling. Find the deepest part of yourself, and see what you feel about this statement.

Acknowledge how you really feel on the most intimate level, and then take a deep, cooling drink of water. Even our most positive emotions can illicit strong and sometimes disturbing responses. Acknowledging you feel them is one way truly to access the Water Element. When you drink the water, you are in effect accepting that you feel what you feel and that is appropriate and okay to do so.

Now do the same things with the three you feel gave you the next-strongest response. Once you have acknowledged them, drink water to accept them. Keep doing this with each of the statements until you have gone through the entire set. This will give you a way of responding to your own feelings that lets them be open and accessible to you.

It is extremely important that you do not judge yourself about what you feel. While you might lean toward feeling guilty about some of your deepest emotions, I encourage you to remember that they are all a part of you. If you deny or negate them, you are essentially denying yourself. While it might not be appropriate to act on some of those stronger emotions, this does not mean they should be ignored or denied. If you are to accept your whole emotional self, you will need to work on accepting all of the parts of you, even the parts that might yield intense responses.

Regardless of whether your feelings are expected or accepted by society, they are your feelings. As such, it is best to acknowledge them and accept them as part of you. Will you at some point release some of these feelings and let them go? Yes. If today is not the day to do that, however, that is just fine. It is as it should be, because that is how it is right now. Although this might be difficult to accept in the moment, it is the best way to acknowledge and embrace your whole emotional self.

4. Water Mission: Wade Into a Body of Water

This Mission will literally take you into the water. This will require a bit of planning on your part, since it might necessitate a trip if you are inclined to make one. Since these Missions are all about what you do for yourself, you will decide how much you are willing or able to do. In an effort to connect most intimately with Water, its fluidity and rhythm, I will ask you to go to a body of water. If it is possible for it to be a natural body of water, that would be terrific, yet a pool is fine for the purpose of this Mission.

Once you get there, take some moments and appreciate the water. Become aware of how it flows. In some ways, it is one giant drop of water held by the shores of its boundaries. Notice its motion, whether it is waves made by the tide or by other swimmers. Pay attention to how it moves and fills what contains it. The water might be a simple swimming pool or a bathtub, or might be a lake, a river, or a mighty ocean. Regardless, please remember that the pull of the moon creates the tides of the oceans.

The tides swell and recede, and are very much like our own emotions as they grow and subside. When we have strong feelings, for example, we might call them the tide of emotions. Or, you might hear the poetical phrase, "His heart overflowed with love." Much Water imagery has been used in love poetry and prose. Many have known just how much Water and emotion are related. The Sufi poet Rumi (1207–1273 CE) wrote, "Love is the Water of Life." I believe he might have meant this figuratively, but this only strengthens the connection between water and emotion.

Now, let us make this connection in the most literal sense. Go to your body of water and slowly, step by step, wade in. Wade into the water until it is about waist deep. Do this gently, and feel each new motion of the water as it brushes by you and simultaneously begins to cradle and buoy you. You will feel a bit lighter and more fluid yourself as you begin to get used to being in this new space. Some of you might have some fear associated with water, and that is why I only ask you to enter the water until it is waist high. Wade and stand still. Keep your focus on how the water moves with and around you. Let your arms relax at your sides, and then relax them until they begin to float around you. Allow the water to move your arms gently to and fro. Free them and relax them so they can move with the water.

Keep track for yourself of any feelings that come to you during this experience. If you feel an emotion rise up, acknowledge it and accept it. There is nothing to fear here. There is simply feeling, and acceptance. This is where you can allow yourself to perceive the waves of emotion available to you to see and to accept. The emotions that surface are the ones you likely need to feel and acknowledge. Please do not judge yourself for whatever you feel. It is simply a part of your experience here and now. You are taking the time to bring in new light and feeling into your state of being. You can see with new eyes if you allow your perceptions to change based on how they are influenced by new environments, surroundings, and energy.

Water is one of the most powerful forces on Earth, and it is directly related to your feelings and their power. Just as the oceans are powerful, our emotions are powerful as well. Many have followed their hearts to the ends of the earth. The ocean, and water in general, are the gateway to those feelings. We can experience them gently or passionately. We can feel great and small. The important thing is to acknowledge, really acknowledge, and accept that our feelings are part of us and are crucial to our wellbeing. Some of us have long buried our emotions. When we were babies and children, we most certainly expressed ourselves immediately upon needing to do so. However, years of living have masked many people's emotions from them. Here is your chance to access your emotions as you feel gently held, and as you open yourself to your feelings. Let them flow through you and from you. Remember what it was like to feel your feelings and express them as you had them. It is our birthright to be heard in this manner, even if sometimes, the only one that hears our feelings is Water. Be here with yourself in this time and place. Feel your emotions right here, right now. Spend some time simply reveling in what your feelings can teach you about yourself.

When you are ready to leave your body of water, turn back and honor it once again. Take the time to honor the feelings it evinced, and honor yourself for experiencing those feelings. Write them down in your Life Elements Journal on a new page. For the next few weeks, I will ask you to start noticing your feelings as they come up and write them in your Journal. Name them and write about your experience of them so you can increase your awareness of your emotions and how they actually feel to you. This will help you honor yourself in the quality and life of your emotions, and it will bring you closer to your own heart. This way, when you have emotions, you will experience them in the moment, and you will be able to address them from a place that feels like home. Good for you!

Chapter 19
Connect with the Elements Day-to-Day

We have discussed the larger, more purposeful things you can do to cultivate specific Elements. There have been Meditations and Missions that have asked you to stretch yourself and push your limits as you integrate the Elements. These were designed to help access the Elements on a more focused, conscious level. As much as that helps you remember how to consciously cultivate specific Elements when you need them, it is also beneficial to access the Elements on a more subconscious daily level. There are things you can do to keep the Elements in your environment that do not require a specific Meditation or Mission. These activities and symbols will support the Integration Process in slightly less obvious but no less important ways.

One of the best ways to access the different Elements is through the use of color. The Elements can be divided according to the color types in which those Elements come. The most straightforward set of Elements that can focus Elemental energy comes from some of the most basic colors. You will likely remember them from childhood. They are the colors red, yellow, blue, and green. The yellow/light-yellow color family is representative of the Air Element. This color, that represents the color of the sunrise sky, will help you to focus, think, and stay on task. (Classrooms that are painted in yellow encourage learning.)

The color red represents the passion of Fire. It is the color of the burning bonfire. A number of Native American Medicine Wheels also link the color red to Fire. Imagine the glowing coals of a campfire or the setting sun.

Blue represents the cooling, healing, flowing power of Water and green is representative of the trees, plants, and grasses of the Earth Element.

If you are at a place to begin to cultivate Elements in your day-to-day life, then this is one of the best and simplest ways to do that. As an example of incorporating an Element into your day-to-day world, paint one wall in your bedroom the color of the Element you wish to cultivate. If, for example, you want to cultivate Fire, then think about painting a wall red, rust, scarlet, or one of the other colors in the Red family. If you cannot do a paint job, then perhaps a pillow placed on your bed will provide some extra Fire energy. If you want to cultivate Water, you might want to incorporate more blue into your day. If you can, it would also be good to wear the colors you want to cultivate. The next time you go shopping, purchase a shirt in the appropriate color. I will not get into color/season theory here (for that, you might wish to get the book *Color Me Beautiful*), but even if you feel that red does not generally suit you, you might find a shade that is flattering.

Please note: Many of you might find that you have already been incorporating some of these things, ideas, and activities into your lives. As an example, one of my life-coaching clients took the EDAT assessment and found she had almost no Fire in her makeup. She was also attempting to find the right life partner for herself. She had spent time dating, and was now ready to locate the grand passion of her life. One of the issues was that she kept finding men who thought she was not passionate or committed enough for them. She realized she wanted to access some of her heretofore hidden passionate nature, and therefore cultivate Fire. We began to talk about some of the things she might do to help her bring Fire's passion into her life. One of the things I suggested is that she might paint a wall in her home a bright, cheery red. She replied that she had her entire house done in reds of one sort or another. She was already instinctively attempting to cultivate more Fire into her life. Once we spoke of this and she began to look at her attempts more consciously, she was able to begin to soak up some of that passion and make it more her own. Rather, I should say she began to use and express some of the passion that had been waiting to be freed.

Incidentally, she did meet a wonderful man, they are truly in love, and as of this writing, they are planning on marrying.

The following will be some ideas on what you might do with color to promote a particular Element in your day-to-day life.

To promote Earth: Bring browns, tans, and greens into your life. You might drape a sarong over your bed, or buy a shirt or blouse in one of those colors. You might also simply draw/doodle in those colors on a piece of paper. Let your imagination run wild as you make swoops and swirls and shapes of any kind in rich, deep earth tones. Then, as a tribute to your artistic endeavor, put up your wonderful piece on the refrigerator. I will ask you to refrain from judging yourself on the quality of your drawing. Simply acknowledge that it was something you created, and take pride in your accomplishment.

Another quick method of cultivating the Earth Element day to day is to begin going for short walks in your neighborhood. Notice the trees and plants that abound where you live. You might even want to take the *Peterson's Guide to Useful Plants* or one of the flower-identification guides on your journeys. You might also wish to get a plant and care for it. (Remember, if you have pets, make sure it is a plant that is not poisonous to them.)

You might also want to begin a collection of rocks or pebbles. If you do begin collecting them, place them around your house so you have them as touchstones when you need some Earth energy. This practice of keeping touchstones around is an old one. People have kept worry stones in their pockets for years, and I believe this is for the exact same goal of bringing peace and grounding to those who might be worried or anxious.

Also, there are certain animals that evince Earth energy. Some of these are: bears, wolves, elephants, sheep, pigs, cows, and snakes. You might find you have already been drawn to these animals. In that case, begin to pay special attention to them in your daily routine. If you wish to be even more proactive, you might even want to get involved in conservation efforts regarding these animals. With your efforts, you will bring their energy into your life: the solidity of the elephant, the protectiveness of the bear, the home-and-hearth quality of sheep and cows, and the loyalty and pragmatism of the wolf. They will help you ground and center even as you move forward in your life.

To promote Air day to day: Bring yellows, light blues, whites, and creams into your life. These colors allow for clarity of vision while they provide either backdrop or illumination. Wear white or yellow shirts. Drape a yellow sarong, or get some fabric remnants in that color family. You might also wish to get wind chimes and place them in a window where you will hear them. Their bright ringing tones will bring the Air Element into your world while you listen to the wind speak through them.

You might want to spend some time drawing with the colors of air, ivory, yellows, light blues, or you might read or write stories or poetry. You might also want to burn incense and spend some time gazing at the smoke as it curls off the incense stick. Rise early and listen to birdsong. Watch the dawn. If you are lucky enough to find a feather on the ground, keep it and place it on a dresser so you can easily see it as often as you like. Take time to watch the sky. Notice its colors and the clouds that float along it.

There are certain animals that evince Air energy. Birds of just about any kind represent Air. You might already have an affinity to eagles, hawks, doves, falcons, chickadees, or other birds. You might find you have already been drawn to these animals, and might have pictures or images of them. In that case, begin to pay special attention to them in your daily routine. If you wish to be even more proactive, you might want to get involved in conservation efforts regarding these animals. When you bring their energy into your life, you will be increasing your affinity with the clarity of their energy, the clear vision of the hawk, the honesty of the eagle's hunt, the purity of purpose of the falcon's soaring flight. These wonderful creatures will help you gain clarity and wisdom.

To promote Water: Incorporate blues, greens, teals, silvers, and turquoises into your life. Art that represents water, like some of the lovely works by the Pre-Raphaelites, might be a good place to start. Place some seashells on your shelves. Grow a plant using hydroponics. Wear those beautiful blues and teals. Paint a wall a bright, cheerful blue. Change your bedspread to one that is blue. Paint or draw with these colors, and hang the result on your refrigerator to honor your artistic achievement. Make or listen to music. Sing along to the radio. Incorporate swimming into your workout regimen. Find time to take a bath instead of showering.

There are certain animals that evince Water energy. We think of fish immediately, but there are others like lobster, oysters, sharks, whales, and dolphins. Together, these animals can run the gamut of human emotion. Think of the happiness of the dolphin's smile and the protectiveness of the blue whale. The majesty and danger of sharks and killer whales represent Water beautifully. All of these will bring about some form of just about any kind of Water energy. The deadly beauty of some of the giant squid and octopi also bring to mind the vast possibility of Water. You might have already realized your affinity for dolphins or whales, and you might want to also look at your connection to some of the other emotions that can be elicited by these amazing creatures.

You might find you have already been drawn to these animals, and you might have pictures or images of them already. In that case, begin to pay special attention to them in your daily routine. If you wish to be even more proactive, you might even want to get involved in conservation efforts regarding these animals. When you bring their energy more into your life, you will be increasing your affinity with the fluidity of their energy: the delight of the dolphin, the peace of the whale, and the unfailing intuition of the shark. These majestic creatures will help you gain access to your feelings even as you move forward in your life.

To promote Fire: Incorporate reds, oranges, and golds into your life. The flames inherent in these colors will shine through and promote Fire's passion, creativity, and forward motion.

Once again, the ideas of painting a wall a fiery red or of changing part of your wardrobe to match the color of the Element you wish to promote would work well. You might notice that a red shirt you have purchased will rapidly become one of your favorite pieces of clothing. You can wear it when you need the passion and conviction of Fire, or if you need to bolster your own momentum.

So, for example, if you need to incorporate Fire, you might wear a red shirt or tie to an interview. Conversely, if you need to stop or end something and you feel trepidatious, you might wish to wear red then as well. It is no surprise that a red tie is considered a "power tie." Red has always been the color of confidence and assertiveness, which are characteristics of the Fire Element.

You will also want to move your body to cultivate Fire. Be active. Play a sport. Go for a brisk walk or a run. Dance. Light candles. Red, orange, or gold candles will doubly evince Fire and help you gain a dose of daily confidence.

There are certain animals that evince Fire energy. This might be a bit more challenging than the obvious animals for Water, but actually, imagine the animals that are the most active in quick motion. The big cats of Africa are quite full of Fire energy. Like Fire, they hunt and destroy to create something new. So, lions, tigers, cheetahs, mountain lions, jaguars, and the other big cats are all Fire animals. Salamanders and chameleons are also Fire animals, for their speed and ability to change. You might find you have already been drawn to these animals, and you might have pictures or images of them already. In that case, begin to pay special attention to them in your daily routine. If you wish to be even more proactive, you might even want to get involved in conservation efforts regarding these animals. When you bring their energy more into your life, you will be increasing your affinity with the passion of their energy: the speed and agility of the cheetah, the keen instincts of the lioness, the strike of the jaguar, and the transformative powers of the chameleon. These majestic creatures will help you access your passionate self.

The above are just some ideas on how you might bring the Elements into your daily life. There are many more ways, and I will explore them in subsequent books and materials. (Check the Life Elements website for updates.) However, right now is your chance to explore. Discover new ways to incorporate aspects of the Elements into your life. Are there foods that will bring the Elements to your life? What are they? List them, and seek them out. Find recipes that are hot and spicy to cultivate Fire. Drink more fluids to cultivate Water. Breathe deeply. Meditate. As you move forward, new things will come to you, and you will begin to experiment. Have fun with this. Enjoy this time of exploration and discovery, because it is simply for you.

Chapter 20
What Happens Next?

First, I want to congratulate you on your journey. I hope you are taking pride in how far you have come. And yet . . .

What happens now? You have taken the EDAT and EIAT. You have discovered your Element Designation(s), and you have cultivated the rest of the Elements so they are becoming more available to you day to day. The Element Integration Process has been all about awakening the inherent peace, passion, emotion, and mindfulness we all possess. These characteristics have been with us since the beginning of our lives. It is just that some of them have become more prominent, depending on which stimuli affected us most as we were growing up. With Life Elements, we have sought and found these other, hidden parts of ourselves so we can be whole and move forward with the strength of all the Elements available to us. Now, with the awareness you have gleaned from the Missions and Meditations, you are much better equipped to do just that: move forward from a place of wholeness and integration.

Once you have completed the Missions and Meditations, you will have a much greater awareness of the roles the Elements can play in your life. I want to assure you that if it does not become second nature right away, that is perfectly fine. These patterns did not become ingrained overnight, and they will not change overnight. Now armed with the knowledge you have gained, however, you can make conscious choices about how you will be, think, feel, and act in whatever situations arise.

As you begin to move forward with the Elements as guides, you will increasingly access them when you need to do so. However, until they are easily available, you will have to be more deliberate in your actions and interactions so you can choose how you will act or react. One way to do this is to take a step back in whatever situation you find yourself. Take a deep breath and analyze what is going on, how you feel, what you think, and how you might act. In other words, take the time to figure out what the Elements are telling you about where you are, and then decide which Element would best serve to point you in the right direction.

Then, once you have decided which Element would be ideal, take a moment and access that Element, by either doing a quick Meditation to it, or by drinking water for Water, by moving around for Fire, by breathing deeply for Air, or by playing with a stone or rock for a few seconds for Earth. As you do so, look inside to find what you can do with the Element's strength, and how you might act or react to what is currently happening. You will likely find a way forward, and then you can do so from your own integrated perspective.

If, for example, you are faced with an issue at work and you have to think and act quickly, it might require that you access the thoughtful nature of Air and then the active nature of Fire so you can proceed appropriately.

Remember, all of the Elements are accessible to you now, and you will choose which to use from your whole, integrated perspective.

Honor Your Completion of the Integration Process

Note: If you have Internet connectivity, go to http://www. LifeElements.info. Click the "Meditations" button (the password is "peace" without the quotes) and click the link "Meditation To Honor Your Completion Of The Integration Process."

As I have stated before, it might be a while before you are consciously aware of the internal transformation that has taken place. Or, you might find you begin to see changes almost immediately in the way you approach your life choices. Regardless, as we have been working with symbols for much of this book, here is one last symbolic ceremony I will ask you to do. This ceremony honors the culmination of all of your efforts and achievements in this process.

You have worked to integrate the Elements, and now it is the time to honor yourself and the Elements as they reside in you.

Find time where you will not be disturbed. You will need approximately fifteen minutes for this last Meditation.

Play some soft, meditative music (There is some music available on the LifeElements website. Go to http://www. LifeElements.info/Missions.htm and click the "Honor the Integration Process Meditation Music" link.)

Gather the following items on a table: a glass full of water, a candle, some incense (or a feather), and a stone or a plant. Lay these objects on the table in a pattern that pleases your eye.

Sit comfortably in front of your table. Close your eyes. Take three deep breaths. On the third exhalation, make an *Ah* sound. Allow your *Ah* to ring strong and true as you gather your energy inside yourself. Let this be a Meditation to yourself as you breathe deeply. When you feel peaceful and calm, open your eyes and look at each of the representations of Earth, Air, Fire, and Water.

Light the incense, and then blow on it to release the curling smoke. Move your hand through the incense smoke, or pick up the feather and gently wave it around. Say the words, "I honor my clarity of thought and mindfulness."

Put down the feather and light the candle. While you watch the flame, say the words, "I honor my passion and creativity."

Take a drink of the water and say the words, "I honor my feelings, intuition, and compassion."

Hold the rock or touch the leaves of the plant and say the words, "I honor my center and my stable foundation."

Put down the rock and say the words, "I honor all of these, as they are part of me." Take the time to feel each of the Elements inside you. They are truly a part of you now.

Breathe three more deep breaths, douse the candle and the incense, and drink the remainder of the water. You have now completed the Life Elements Integration Process. Congratulations, and as the Aussies would say, "Good onya."

My Last Few Words

When you first started on this path, you were likely guided by only one or perhaps two Elements. Generally, you had certain patterns you tended to follow, and other modes of thought or behavior remained elusive. Now that you have taken the time to acquaint yourself with the other Elements, I imagine that new patterns are emerging in your life. Whereas before you might have leapt before you looked or over analyzed every situation, now you might be finding you have a calmer center, a place you can go to seek your own inner wisdom. The Earth Element's ability to center and stabilize has likely become more accessible to you. It is also possible you have begun to trust that inner knowing that comes from cultivation of Water. Whichever Elements you have cultivated to complete the Integration Process, you are now in a better position to approach the rest of your path.

Where might this lead? For some, the fulfillment of the first four Elements leads to the fifth: Spirit. You might find that as your own peace, contentment, and happiness increase, you are more open to the other wonders. You might find joy in the simplest of thoughts and activities, because they come from a conscious place where you love and accept yourself first and foremost. Once you are in this place, you might also wish to help others find their path there as well. You might find you enjoy your life sufficiently to seek other, more spiritual pursuits, or you might wish simply to be at peace. At this point, I feel it is entirely up to your individual choices. As long as you approach your life from this integrated place, you will maintain balance among the four Elements.

Instead of finding Spirit, other people choose the path of seeking. They keep looking and moving forward. I find this a wonderful path, as long as the person on it walks from a place of certainty and integration. Once the Elements are integrated, everything is truly a possibility. At this point, you might wish to ask yourself what you really want. What are your goals? Now that you can look at them with clarity of vision and peace and an emotional center, you can begin to clarify for yourself exactly what you wish to achieve. Here is where you can identify what will bring you long-term happiness, and you can move to achieve from a place of awareness and wholeness. What a wonderful place to be!

Some of you might want to delve deeper into the Elemental mysteries and the intricacies of the Integration Process. Certainly, there are more of these mysteries to explore, and I encourage you to do so. Some of these might involve getting into yoga or Tai Chi, or some other internal practices or activities that encompass and incorporate the Elements. Some of it might involve your own internal exploration while you continue to delve deeper into your own identity, emotions, and self. I will create more of these Missions and Meditations, and you will also discover some.

Follow your interests as they lead you. Remember to check in with all four major parts of yourself. See how you feel, what you think, and whether or not you are at peace before you act, and once all four of those are in accord, you will walk your path creatively and authentically. I could not wish for any more than that.

Yours in Earth, Air, Fire, and Water,
Izolda

Bibliography

Anand, Margot, *The Art of Everyday Ecstasy: The Seven Tantric Keys for Bringing Passion, Spirit, and Joy into Every Part of Your Life.* New York: Broadway Books, a division of Random House, Inc., 1999.

Benson, Tom, *What Is Thermodynamics?* National Aeronautics and Space Administration: http://www.grc.nasa.gov/WWW/K-12/airplane/thermo.html

Blood, Peter, Patterson, Annie, *Rise Up, Singing.* Bethlehem, PA: Sing Out Corp., 1992.

Bruser, Madeline, *The Art of Practicing: A Guide to Making Music from the Heart.* New York: Harmony/Bell Tower, 1997.

Bunning, Joan, *Learning the Tarot: An Online Course.* http://www.learntarot.com/

Cameron, Julia, *The Artist's Way: A Spiritual Path to Higher Creativity.* New York: G.P. Putnam's Sons, 1992.

Chopra, Deepak, *The Book of Secrets: Unlocking the Hidden Dimensions of Your Life.* New York: Harmony Books, 2004

Dollar, Cindy, MacKenzie Euston, Susanna, *Yoga Your Way: Customizing Your Home Practice.* New York: Serling Publishing Co., Inc. 2004

Edwards, Betty, *Drawing on the Right Side of the Brain: A Course in Enhancing Creativity and Artistic Confidence.* New York: Penguin Putnam, Inc. 1999.

Gawain, Shakti, *Creative Visualization.* San Rafael, CA: Bantam Books, New World Library. 1978.

Iyengar, B.K.S., *Light on Yoga.* New York: Shocken Books, Inc.1979.

James, William, The Principles of Psychology, 2 vols. (1890) Dover Publications, 1950.

Judith, Anodea, *Eastern Body Western Mind: Psychology and the Chakra System as a Path to the Self.* Berkeley, CA: Celestial Arts Publishing, 1996.

Marks, Kate, *Circle of Song: Songs, Chants, and Dances for Ritual and Celebration.* Lenox, MA: Full Circle Press, 1993.

Milman, Dan, *Way of the Peaceful Warrior: A Book That Changes Lives.* Tiburon, CA: H.J. Kramer, Inc., 1984.

Yee, Rodney, *Moving Toward Balance: 8 Weeks of Yoga with Rodney Yee.* Emmaus, PA: Rodale, 2004.

About the Author

Born in Moldova in the former Soviet Union, Izolda grew up steeped in the rich heritage of Eastern Europe. When she was six, her family immigrated to the USA. During the year-plus immigration process, they lived in Israel and Italy where Izolda soaked up those cultures and languages. The family settled in Michigan where she graduated from the University of Michigan.

As Director of Writing and Production for The Information Prospector, she gained invaluable experience in interpersonal relations, societal trends and tendencies, and the human mind. The Information Prospector conducted public records research reports on successful individuals for philanthropic purposes. While developing and producing these reports, she learned much about the manner in which successful people achieve their goals. That knowledge planted the seeds of the Life Elements System's focus on self-directed success. Izolda worked at both the National Geographic Society and then NASA where she worked for the GLOBE Program. Envisioned by Vice President Al Gore in his book, Earth In The Balance, the GLOBE Program is a unique international partnership among students, teachers, and scientists where students study the earth and care for the environment. Izolda honed her teaching and training skills in workshops as she developed the training methodology for the Soil protocols and then traveled the world as a Master Trainer in the Atmosphere, Land Cover, Hydrology, and Soil protocols. This knowledge, these skills and her interest in ancient symbolism and methodologies further developed her insight into human interactions and tendencies. She saw the patterns and relationships among self-directed change, self-confidence, and ancient Elemental/environmental symbolism and synthesized them into the Life Elements System.

An award-winning educator, she developed and taught a series of "Learn to Sing" classes and incorporated an inquiry-based teaching style with traditional vocal technique, aesthetics and mechanics. These classes help participants discover and develop their voices and find joy in singing. They also help students connect with others, express themselves creatively, raise their self-confidence, and achieve long-sought goals. These classes and her private teaching sparked her thoughts on Therapeutic Creativity and the ability of creative pursuits to help in individual and societal healing. She currently teaches "Finding Your Sacred Voice" and "Workin' Harmony" singing and team building workshops at both corporate and festival events.

Izolda has also studied the ancient energy workings of Reiki and Chi energy. She has been a Tai Chi practitioner and teacher for over 13 years, a yoga practitioner for seven years, and she is also a certified Reiki practitioner. She opened the Healer's Arts Wellness Center in September 2005. The Wellness Center follows and teaches the Life Elements System where Izolda provides energy healing and holistic life coaching.

An accomplished musician, Izolda released her CD "Sound the Deep Waters" in 2003. She and her husband reside in Greenbelt, MD with their three cats, and a house full of musical instruments and juggling clubs.

Index

A

Y

Z

Healer's Arts Publishing
The Elements of Life

Upcoming Publications:
Life Elements Journal and Workbook
Life Elements Mini-Mission Card Pack

Order Form

To order online, go to http://LifeElements.info/shop.htm
To order by mail, send a copy of this order form to:
Healer's Arts Publishing
PO Box 1133, Greenbelt, MD 20768

Please send the following books or other materials:

_____

_____

Name:_____

Address: _____

City: _____ State: _____ Zip: _____

Phone (with area code): _____

Email:_____

Sales tax: Please add 6% for products shipped to Maryland addresses.

Shipping: US: $4 for the first product and $2 for each additional product. International: $9 for first product; $5 for each additional (estimate)

Payment: ☐ Check (enclose check), ☐ Visa ☐ Mastercard

Card number: _____

Name on card:_____ Exp. date: _____/ _____

Three-digit security code from back of card: _____

Please check the Life Elements website for new books, cards, and other supplemental materials. http://LifeElements.info